T0358630

Team Academy in Diverse Settings

Within Entrepreneurship Education, Team Academy (TA) is seen by some as an innovative pedagogical model that enhances social connectivity, as well as experiential, student-centred, and team-based learning. It also creates spaces for transformative learning to occur.

This fourth book of the Routledge Focus on Team Academy book series the TA model is examined outside of the traditional TA-based settings (industry, schools, communities of practice, etc.) in different countries (Brazil, Japan, UK, Finland, Argentina, Tanzania, Spain, etc.). The legacy that this has left in learners and practitioners who have engaged with the model is also explored.

This book is aimed at academics, practitioners, and learners engaged in the Team Academy methodology, pedagogy, and model, as well as those interested in the area of entrepreneurial team learning. Readers will be inspired to innovate in their delivery methodologies and to explore learning-by-doing approaches to creating value. The book also aims to challenge the discourse around entrepreneurship and entrepreneurial activities, offering insights, research, stories, and experiences from those learning and working in the Team Academy approach.

Dr. Berrbizne Urzelai is Team Coach and Senior Lecturer in areas of International Management and Entrepreneurship at the University of the West of England, UK.

Dr. Elinor Vettraino is Head Coach and Programme Director of the Business Enterprise Development portfolio at Aston University, UK.

Routledge Focus on Team Academy
Series Editors—Berrbizne Urzelai and Elinor Vettraino

Higher Education organizations (HE) operate in an environment that continuously pushes towards innovation by educators. From this perspective, Team Academy is seen as an innovative pedagogical model that enhances social connectivity, as well as experiential, student-centred and team-based learning. It also creates spaces for transformative learning to occur.

Since its creation in Finland in 1993, the number of institutions adopting this approach has been expanding in many parts of Europe and beyond, and it is increasingly attracting the interest of organizations that want to adopt a model that emphasizes on the transversal competences and skills acquired by its entrepreneurial learners. The aim of this series is to compile the different research, experiences, and stories about the Team Academy phenomenon throughout its worldwide network.

The audience of the books is multidisciplinary, directed to academics and practitioners. Entrepreneurial education and research has traditionally been focused on the individual entrepreneur. However, in the current business scenario, entrepreneurs' teamwork efforts, social capital, and networking skills are essential to face the entrepreneurial issues and challenges that they currently face. The books adopt a Team Academy pedagogical approach that focuses on critical factors such as team and experiential learning, leadership, or entrepreneurial mindset, which makes this collection a key information source for those looking at new directions of entrepreneurship education and practice.

Team Academy and Entrepreneurship Education
Edited by Elinor Vettraino and Berrbizne Urzelai

Team Academy in Practice
Edited by Berrbizne Urzelai and Elinor Vettraino

Team Academy Leadership and Teams
Edited by Elinor Vettraino and Berrbizne Urzelai

Team Academy in Diverse Settings
Edited by Berrbizne Urzelai and Elinor Vettrain

Team Academy in Diverse Settings

Edited by Berrbizne Urzelai and Elinor Vettraino

Routledge
Taylor & Francis Group

NEW YORK AND LONDON

First published 2022
by Routledge
605 Third Avenue, New York, NY 10158

and by Routledge
4 Park Square, Milton Park, Abingdon, Oxon, OX14 4RN

Routledge is an imprint of the Taylor & Francis Group, an informa business

© 2022 selection and editorial matter, Berrbizne Urzelai and Elinor Vettraino; individual chapters, the contributors

The right of Berrbizne Urzelai and Elinor Vettraino to be identified as the authors of the editorial material, and of the authors for their individual chapters, has been asserted in accordance with sections 77 and 78 of the Copyright, Designs and Patents Act 1988.

All rights reserved. No part of this book may be reprinted or reproduced or utilised in any form or by any electronic, mechanical, or other means, now known or hereafter invented, including photocopying and recording, or in any information storage or retrieval system, without permission in writing from the publishers.

Trademark notice: Product or corporate names may be trademarks or registered trademarks, and are used only for identification and explanation without intent to infringe.

Library of Congress Cataloging-in-Publication Data
Names: Urzelai, Berrbizne, editor. | Vettraino, Elinor, editor.
Title: Team academy in diverse settings / edited by Dr. Berrbizne
    Urzelai and Dr. Elinor Vettraino.
Description: New York, NY : Routledge, 2022. | Series: Routledge
    focus on team academy | Includes bibliographical references
    and index.
Identifiers: LCCN 2021048017 (print) | LCCN 2021048018 (ebook) |
    ISBN 9780367756017 (hardback) | ISBN 9780367756048 (paperback) |
    ISBN 9781003163176 (ebook)
Subjects: LCSH: Teams in the workplace—Management. |
    Organizational behavior. | Organizational sociology.
Classification: LCC HD66 .T41745 2022 (print) |
    LCC HD66 (ebook) | DDC 658.4/022—dc23
LC record available at https://lccn.loc.gov/2021048017
LC ebook record available at https://lccn.loc.gov/2021048018

ISBN: 978-0-367-75601-7 (hbk)
ISBN: 978-0-367-75604-8 (pbk)
ISBN: 978-1-003-16317-6 (ebk)

DOI: 10.4324/9781003163176

Typeset in Times New Roman
by Apex CoVantage, LLC

For all the challengers, change makers, and future thinkers on the planet.

—Dr. Berrbizne Urzelai

For Elvis, who still struggles with coaching!

—Dr. Elinor Vettraino

Table of Contents

Figures

Tables

Acknowledgements

We would like to thank all of the contributors for their stories, and the learners, researchers, and practitioners for their commitment to exploration and learning-by-doing. Without them, this book wouldn't have been possible.

Dr. Berrbizne Urzelai and Dr. Elinor Vettraino

Contributors

Editors

Berrbizne Urzelai
Team Coach and Senior Lecturer, University of West of England, UK

Dr. Berrbizne Urzelai is a team coach and senior lecturer at the University
of the West of England (UWE), Bristol, UK. Her teaching and research
work is on Strategic Management, International Business and Entrepreneurship. She holds an international PhD (Hons) degree in Economics
and Business Management (University of Valencia), an MSc degree in
East Asian Studies (University of Bristol), and an MBA (Mondragon
University). She is also a fellow of HEA. She has experience in working
at different institutions applying TA programmes in different countries.
Her research is related to international business, agglomeration economies, social capital, and knowledge management, as well as TA-related
country and model comparisons. Her research has received several
awards (best paper 2017 XXVII ACEDE, best doctoral communication 2015 Torrecid, PhD scholarship, etc.). She is a member of different
research groups, GESTOR (Organizational Geostrategy: Clusters and
Competitiveness) at the University of Valencia and BLCC (Bristol Leadership and Change Centre) at UWE. For her publications, see https://
people.uwe.ac.uk/Person/Berrbizne2Urzelai.

Elinor Vettraino
Programme Director and Head Coach, Aston University, UK

Dr. Elinor Vettraino is a head coach and programme director of the Business
Enterprise Development portfolio at Aston University, Birmingham, UK
She also leads the Aston Business Clinic. She is a founder and director
of Active Imagining, an organizational development and leadership consultancy. She is also a director of Akatemia UK through which she runs
training for academics, consultants, and practitioners who are developing a programme of learning based on the principles of the TA model.

Elinor has a DEd Psychology (University of Dundee) and is a principal fellow of HEA and a chartered fellow/chartered manager of CMI. Her research is currently based on understanding how the TA model supports transformational learning for participants and how the application of arts-based pedagogies might support the development of negative capability in team coaches and team entrepreneurs.

Contributors

Duncan Iraci
Team coach and Senior Lecturer, University of the West of England, UK

Duncan is a team coach on the (BA Hons) Business – Team Entrepreneurship degree at UWE. He is.currently in his 6th year on the program. He has a Product Design Technology BSc (Hons) 1st Class and is an Executive MBA. His background is in product design, branding, and graphics with extensive experience in events and exhibitions and working with start-ups. He is currently also a director of a property management company based in Bristol.

Berrbizne Urzelai
Team Coach and Senior Lecturer, University of West of England, UK

Dr. Berrbizne Urzelai is Team Coach and Senior Lecturer at the University of the West of England (UWE), Bristol (UK). Her teaching and research work is on Strategic Management, International Business and Entrepreneurship. She holds an international PhD (Hons) in Economics and Business Management (University of Valencia), an MSc in East Asian Studies (University of Bristol) and an MBA (Mondragon University). She is also a Fellow of HEA. She has experience in working at different institutions applying Team Academy programmes in different countries. Her research is related to international business, agglomeration economies, social capital, and knowledge management as well as TA-related country and model comparisons. Her research has received several awards (best paper 2017 XXVII ACEDE, best doctoral communication 2015 Torrecid, PhD. Scholarship, etc.). She is a member of different research groups, GESTOR (Organizational Geostrategy: Clusters and Competitiveness) at the University of Valencia and BLCC (Bristol Leadership and Change Centre) at UWE.

Georgina Dance
Senior Lecturer, University of West of England, UK

Georgina Dance is one of the founders of the Team Entrepreneurship (TE) programme at the University of the West of England (UWE) and Link

Tutor and Coaching Supervisor for the Sports Business and Entrepreneurship programme at the Bristol City Robins Foundation. She began her work with Team Academy in 2012 developing the UWE programme and has since Team Coached multiple teams, most recently the TE Law Teams. Her leading role on TE is now as the Coaching Supervisor for the Team Coaches. She is a senior lecturer and both a UWE Learning and Teaching Fellow and a Fellow of The Higher Education Academy and works on multiple experiential modules at UWE in both the Business and Law school where she uses coaching to underpin her work with learners and Coaching Supervision to underpin her work with staff.

Georgiana Els
Senior Lecturer in Tourism and Events Management, University of Lincoln, UK

Dr. Georgiana Els (Ciuchete) is Senior Lecturer in Tourism and Events Management at Lincoln International Business School (LIBS) and the Departmental Director of Teaching and Learning. She joined the team in 2013 after previously working and collaborating with Salford Business School (Manchester), Romanian American University and Academy of Economic Studies (Bucharest). Georgiana has been awarded magna cum laude for her doctorate in 2012 following several years of management experience in the travel and tourism industry. Her business experience enabled opportunities to work internationally and to train as a Team Academy team coach. Georgiana's current role with LIBS involves teaching and coaching, research, programme leadership and development, international partnerships and citizenship. In 2019 she was awarded a Teaching Excellence Award from the Vice Chancellor and the Senior Leadership Team.

Tuula Koivukangas
Teacher and team Coach, City of Kuopio, Finland

Tuula Koivukangas is a class teacher and team coach. She has worked as a team coach for the Parasta ennen project in 21 primary schools in the Northern Savonia region of Finland. The project was awarded a prize by the National Board of Education. Tuula has also worked as a developer teacher and trainer in co-operation between pre-school and primary education. She is currently working as a primary school teacher at Martti Ahtisaari Primary School in Kuopio, Finland. Tuula's mission is to work for a humane and team-learning school by inviting people to dialogue.

Päivi Rimpiläinen
Special education teacher and Team Coach, City of Kuopio, Finland

Päivi Rimpiläinen is a special education teacher and team coach. She has been doing in-service training for teaching staff for more than 20 years.

She has worked as a team coach for the Parasta ennen project in 21 primary schools in the Northern Savonia region of Finland. The project was awarded a prize by the National Board of Education. Päivi is currently working as a special teacher at Martti Ahtisaari Primary School in Kuopio, Finland. Päivi's mission is to work for a humane and team-learning school by inviting people to dialogue.

Wendy Wu
Business Adviser and Lecturer of Entrepreneurship and Innovation, Edinburgh Napier University, UK

Dr. Wendy Wu has more than 20 years' experience in developing organizations, products, services and businesses. Prior to embarking on an academic path, she was the CEO of a charity and founded various businesses in service industries. She currently has a dual role at Edinburgh Napier University (ENU) – she is both a business adviser and a lecturer in Entrepreneurship and Innovation. As a business adviser she has advised more than 300 businesses from ideation to scale up. As an academic she specialises in change management, entrepreneurship development, philanthropic funding strategy and knowledge transfer. She is also a strong advocate of experiential learning. In 2020 she founded Impact Investment Symposium, which brings together leading investors, academics, social enterprises, philanthropists and other change makers to advance ESG and purpose-driven business. Dr. Wu is also an accredited Team Coach with Tiimiakatemia in Finland and Akatemia in the UK. In her spare time she enjoys writing poetry and walking.

Hock Tan
Lecturer, Edinburgh Napier University, UK

Hock Tan, since joining Edinburgh Napier University, has been involved in two Knowledge Transfer Partnership programmes in the areas of quality management and sustainability. He was a programme leader for BA Business Management (Singapore) and an external examiner at Coventry University. His current area of research is in business strategy and sustainable development. Hock has consistently pursued social innovation in his research and teaching. His most influential contribution to the field was the development of a Knowledge Transfer Project for Innovate UK, establishing a development platform to align Corporate Responsibility Efforts of Businesses to the needs of the Third Sector.

Pauline Miller Judd
Associate Professor, Edinburgh Napier University, UK

Pauline Miller Judd, with 20+ years' experience as a leader in education and creative industries, works with a range of teams to develop new initiatives and challenge existing thinking. Pauline began her career in the arts before moving into higher education and her academic focus is on creative industries and entrepreneurial thinking. Pauline was previously Dean of School of Arts and Creative Industries at Edinburgh Napier University and now combines teaching with freelance coaching and facilitation. Pauline is a qualified Team Academy Coach, a Senior Fellow of the Higher Education Academy (HEA), and leads the NCEE Entrepreneurial Heads of Department programme.

Hajime Imamura
Professor, Department of Global Innovation Studies, Faculty of Global and Regional Studies, Toyo University, Japan

Hajime Imamura is Professor at the Department of Global Innovation Studies (GINOS) of Toyo University teaching courses such as Global Entrepreneurship. Imamura was a Chair of the GINOS and a Deputy Director of the Center for Global Innovation Studies (GIC) from 2017 to 2020, which started as the flagship education and research organization of Toyo University's Top Global University project under MEXT. He has been leading the research and education of creative and innovative human resources with entrepreneurship mindset in Japan. And, he is also the co-founder of CREAPS-DESIGN and promoting Creative Public Space Design in Japan.

Roberta Leme Sogayar
Chief Tourism Officer, Botucatu City Hall, Brazil

Roberta Leme Sogayar holds a PhD degree and a Master's degree in Hospitality, and a Master's degree in Recreation, Parks and Tourism Administration. She is currently the Chief Tourism Officer at the city of Botucatu, where she is promoting initiatives of sustainable tourism and is the Project Manager for Polo Cuesta, a regional instance of tourism development. She worked for almost 20 years as a university teacher within the programs of Tourism, Hospitality, Events and Marketing, and as the Academic Quality Manager. She also held a position of consultant for the Ministry of Education for eight years. She has authored many academic papers in Brazil and is an advocate of Team Academy throughout her life.

Tomás Sparano Martins
Associate Professor, Federal University of Paraná, Brazil

Tomás Sparano Martins holds a PhD degree in Strategy Management from Pontifica Universidade Católica do Paraná. He is currently an associate professor at the Universidade Federal do Paraná, where he coordinates the Marketing Lab, an innovation space for the development of experiential projects based on digital transformation and Team Academy. He is one of the founders of Beecoop, an ecosystem of cooperative learning and transformation that connects experts from several areas to develop innovative solutions for cooperatives and the community at large. He is the author of several academic articles and books in the areas of strategic management and marketing.

Natalia Ceruti
Learning Designer & Catalyst, High Impact Learning. Argentina

Natalia Ceruti believes learning is a superpower. She loves to learn and to catalyse transformational learning experiences. She has more than 25 years of work experience in diverse industries (IT, Agricultural Production, Entertainment, Education, Government). This experience, when added to the academic knowledge on how humans learn, allows her to generate well-founded and at the same time pragmatic holistic proposals. The idea behind her interventions is always to challenge, experiment, collaborate and integrate what is usually disconnected. Nati advises leaders and trains teams in Strategy, Leadership, Team Development, and Personal Development. She designs and implements Programs, Workshops, Events, Change Processes, and Social Innovation Strategies in public organizations and private companies. Her formal academic experience includes a BA in Psychology, a BA in Business Administration, and a Master's degree in Cognitive Psychology and Learning (UAM, Spain). She holds a Diploma in Mediation and Negotiation (IUKB, Switzerland). She is a Tiimiakatemia (Finland) certified Team Coach. She also has certifications in various practices and methodologies 'outside the mainstream' such as Design Thinking, Visual Thinking, Scrum, Appreciative Inquiry, Art of Hosting, Spiral Dynamics and U Theory, among others. As an entrepreneur, she runs High Impact Learning (a company that represents and implements international educational models in Latin America) and Love2Learn (a start-up dedicated to creating learning ecosystems). In addition to that, she has been a permanent Guest Professor at the University of Applied Sciences in Jyväskylä (Finland) for 12 years, where she teaches Psychology programmes for Managers.

Deo Sabokwigina
Director and Head Coach, Centre for Entrepreneurship and Innovation, University of Iringa, Tanzania

Deo Sabokwigina is the Director of the Centre for Entrepreneurship and Innovation (CEI) of which his is a co-founder. He is also a lecturer at the

University of Iringa, Tanzania. He has a passion for empowering university students and graduates in technology, business and entrepreneurship. He was a driving force in establishing a unique and transformative learning by-doing Team Academy programme in Tanzania. He co-founded Kiota Innovation Hub; a space for idea nurturing, mindset transformation, co-creation and networking. In 2015, he was nationally recognized by the Minister of ICT for his contribution to the Innovation Ecosystem in Tanzania.

Ainhoa Esnaola
Co-founder, TAZEBAEZ, Basque Country, Spain

Ainhoa Esnaola is a cooperative member of TAZEBAEZ s.coop and COO of Traveling U, a business initiative of the same company. Graduated from Mondragon Unibertsitatea in Business Leadership and Innovation (2013 / LEINN), and International Master's degree in Intrapreneurship and Open Innovation (2014/MINN), as well as a Master's degree in International Cooperation and Emancipatory Education from the University of the Basque Country (2020). She has worked in several cooperation and education projects for public and private institutions in entrepreneurship, education (formal and non-formal) and innovation, highlighting his time at UWE in Bristol collaborating in the consolidation of the Team Academy methodology and in Korea, co-leading and co-designing the first edition of the pioneering Change Maker Lab program (TU-MTA-SKHU-HBM). Co-founder of the international network of team entrepreneurs Mondragon Team Academy as part of TAZEBAEZ, the first cooperative created as a result of the Mondragon University degree, the first promotion of the first official degree in entrepreneurship (accredited in March 2017).

Joanes Røsø
CEO, TAZEBAEZ, Basque Country, Spain

Joanes Røsø is CEO and President of TAZEBAEZ. Graduated from Mondragon Unibertsitatea in Entrepreneurial Leadership and Innovation (2013/LEINN), and International Master in Intrapreneurship and Open Innovation (2014/MINN) as well as International Team Mastery program for Team Coaches (2018/TMINN) in collaboration with Jyväskylä University of Applied Sciences (Tiimiakatemia Finland). His background and training as a Superior Technician in Restoration (2005/Leioa Hospitality School) and Tourism studies (2007/University of Deusto) is noteworthy. He has co-led several cooperation and strategic consulting projects for both private and public institutions in entrepreneurship, education (formal and non-formal) and innovation. He co-founded the international network of team entrepreneurs Mondragon Team Academy as co-founder of the first cooperative created as a result of the Mondragon University degree, the first promotion of the first official degree in entrepreneurship (accredited in March 2017).

Beth Williams
Team Coach and Managing Director of OKO Marketplace, Bristol City Robins Foundation/ OKO, UK

Beth Williams is a Team Coach at Ashton Gate, Bristol on the Sports & Entrepreneurship degree programme. She is also an entrepreneur currently running a successful online business; OKO Marketplace, where she sells her own range of natural and plastic-free haircare, skincare, and home fragrance products. She holds a First-Class Honours in the Team Entrepreneurship degree programme of which she formed a part of the first every cohort in the UK to graduate from a degree in entrepreneurship. She also holds a Team Mastery Coaching qualification and is currently completing a post-graduate qualification in coaching. She has worked for and with an array of small and large businesses and from this has developed and grown her entrepreneurial mindset.

Introduction
Team Academy in Diverse Settings

Berrbizne Urzelai and Elinor Vettraino

Team Academy: Philosophy, Pedagogy, Process

Within Entrepreneurship Education, Team Academy (TA) is seen by some as an innovative pedagogical model that enhances social connectivity, as well as experiential (Kolb, 1984; Kayes, 2002), student-centred (Brandes & Ginnis, 1986) and team-based learning (Senge, 1990). It also creates spaces for transformative learning to occur (Mezirow, 2008, 1991).

If you really want to see the future of management education, you should see Team Academy (Peter Senge, 2008) made this comment over a decade ago about TA and since its inception in JAMK– the university of applied sciences, Jyväskylä, Finland, in the early 1990s, educators and practitioners engaging in TA-based programmes have continuously pushed at the innovation boundaries of more traditional teaching approaches to education.

TA is often referred to as a model of entrepreneurship education. There are certainly tools, techniques and approaches that are used within the delivery of a TA-based programme that would support the idea of this being a framework or model that can be applied in different contexts. However, TA is a complex concept appearing not just as a model of activity, but as a pedagogical approach to learning and as a process of self (personal and professional) development. As a pedagogical approach, TA draws on the concept of heutagogical learning (Hase & Kenyon, 2001; Blaschke & Hase, 2016) to develop learners' capacity for self-determination in relation, not just to their academic work, but to their entrepreneurial ventures and their personal and professional development.

Since its creation, the number of institutions adopting this approach has been expanding in many parts of Europe and beyond, and it is increasingly attracting the interest of organizations that want to adopt a model that emphasizes the transversal competences and skills acquired by its entrepreneurial learners.

DOI: 10.4324/9781003163176-1

Why This Book Series, and Why Now?

BERRBIZNE: The idea of publishing a Team Academy (TA) book for me started back in 2017 when I began working in the UK, because I could see that there were many differences between how TA was run in Mondragon (Basque Country) and at UWE (UK). In November that year I met with an editor from Routledge and shared some of my ideas which he became excited about. However, it was not until March 2018 that I really started to put some ideas together for the project. I was already in touch with Elinor Vettraino, co-editor of this series, at that time as we were working on several cross-university projects and I remember a conversation I had with her over dinner in Finland in January 2018 (*Timmiakatemia*'s 25th Anniversary). Essentially, we were discussing why it was that not many people knew about TA even within our institutions. How could it be possible that we were not using that amazing global network more effectively?

ELINOR: In June 2018, the Team Academy UK community had their annual meeting event – the TAUK Gathering. During this connection a number of team coaches met and reflected together about how research could actually inform our team coaching practice, programme design, pedagogical thinking, etc. I was keen to organize a Team Learning Conference where we could invite people from TA but also other EE practitioners and academics to present their work and share their knowledge. At this point, Berrbizne and I realized that we had an opportunity to pool our interests together and publish a book for dissemination as well as organize a conference to share knowledge and practice.

BERRBIZNE: I was about to go on maternity leave so I thought . . . this is the moment! I need to do something during this time, so let's work on the book proposal. We created a call for chapters and started reaching out to people from our network to invite them to send us an abstract. The response was great and we ended up working on a proposal that had too many chapters so Routledge suggested a book series instead. We didn't want to leave people out of this so we thought *let's do it!*

The rest, as they say, is history!

The Aim of the Series

Surprisingly there is very little published research about the theory and practice behind the Team Academy model, so this book series aims to change that position.

We have four main objectives through this project:

- Challenge the existing discourse around entrepreneurship, entrepreneurial activities and enterprise education, and act as a provocation to generate new knowledge based on team learning and generating networks of teams.
- Collate research, narratives about practice and the experiences of academics, team coaches and team entrepreneurs who have worked with and through the Team Academy model of learning, and to offer new insights to those engaged in developing entrepreneurial education.
- Inspire academics and practitioners to innovate in their delivery methodologies and to explore learning-by-doing approaches to creating value.
- Show the diversity of approaches that exist within the TA network (different institutions, countries, designs, etc.).

We wanted to compile the different research, experiences, and stories about the Team Academy phenomenon throughout its worldwide network. This included research but also narrative journeys, reflections and student voices. This will allow us to get TA on the map when it comes to research as we wanted to show that because you work in TA doesn't mean you can't be a researcher.

There is not a single TA model as different institutions have applied this approach in different ways, so we wanted to celebrate the diversity within the model and create an international network of practitioners and researchers that work around it. This will not only inform our practice but also offer it externally as something to be explored by other educators, which is different from traditional learning and teaching models.

The Story of *Team Academy in Diverse Settings*

In his quote "It is impossible to export pedagogical practices without reinventing them" Freire (2005, p. x) emphasized the idea that educators should pay careful attention to cultural differences, insisting that education should neither impose nor colonize.

This fourth book of the *Routledge Focus on Team Academy* series focuses on the different contexts and learning environments in which Team Academy pedagogical and cultural practices coalesce.

The reader will find research and narratives about university-based incubators, team coaches' practices in the UK, or the entrepreneurial and team learning path of teachers' teams in primary school settings in Finland. Besides, the book includes stories from alumni from TA programmes that explain how their experience was, and how it shaped their future careers. TZBZ for example is one of those team companies established in the TA programme of Mondragon University (LEINN) in the Basque Country, Spain, which still survives after 10 years as a cooperative enterprise. Among these stories, this book also reflects on how universities, institutions or organizations have adopted some of the elements of the TA methodology to inspire their practices in, for instance, creating an ecosystem for creative innovation and entrepreneurship in Japan, developing interventions with young entrepreneurs in Argentina, or encouraging economic prosperity and change through creation of enterprising graduates that inspire others in Africa. Sometimes the attempts to implement TA methods have turned impossible (i.e. Brazil) and the learning from these experiences tell us more about to what extent TA is replicable in other contexts.

This book therefore offers new insights to those engaged in developing entrepreneurial education from stories and reflections that show the diversity of approaches that exist around the world about how Team Academy inspired models of learning operate, and towards which settings TA may move in the future.

References

Blaschke, L. M., & Hase, S. (2016). Heutagogy: A holistic framework for creating 21st century self-determined learners. In B. Gros & M. Maina Kinshuk (Eds.), *The future of ubiquitous learning: Learning designs for emerging pedagogies* (pp. 25–40). New York City: Springer.

Brandes, D., & Ginnis, P. (1986). *A guide to student centred learning*. Oxford: Blackwell.

Freire, P. (2005). *Teachers as cultural workers, letters to those who dare teach* (D. Macedo, D. Koike, & A. Oliveira, Trans.). Boulder, CO: Westview Press.

Hase, S., & Kenyon, C. (2001). Moving from andragogy to heutagogy: Implications for VET. In Proceedings of Research to Reality: Putting VET Research to Work: Australian Vocational Education and Training Research Association (AVETRA), Adelaide, SA, 28–30 March. Crows Nest, NSW: AVETRA.

Kayes, D. C. (2002). Experiential learning and its critics: Preserving the role of experience in management learning and education. *Academy of Management Learning & Education, 1*(2), 137–149. https://doi.org/10.5465/amle.2002.8509336

Kolb, D. A. (1984). *Experiential learning: Experience as the source of learning and development*. Englewood Cliffs, NJ: Prentice-Hall.

Mezirow, J. (1991). *Transformative dimensions of adult learning*. San Francisco, CA: Jossey-Bass.

Mezirow, J. (2008). An overview on transformative learning. *Lifelong learning*, 40–54..

Senge, P. (1990), *The Fifth Discipline: The Art and Practice of the Learning Organization,* Doubleday, New York, NY.

Senge, P. (2008). *Peter Senge—Team Academy*. Tiimiakatemia Global Ltd., Youtube channel.

1 Team Coaching Practice in the UK, a Comparative Study

Duncan Iraci, Berrbizne Urzelai, and Georgina Dance

The Role and Practice of Team Academy (TA) Team Coaching (TCg)

There is little agreement on a clear definition of coaching or how it differs to the discipline of mentoring (Cox et al., 2018; Clutterbuck, 2013; Garvey et al., 2017). Although a number of coaching disciplines are acknowledged including career coaching (Yates, 2013), life coaching (Neenan & Dryden, 2013), sports coaching (Lyle & Cushion, 2016) and business coaching (Cox et al., 2018).

Team, group and leadership coaching literature (Thornton, 2016; Hawkins, 2017; Cox et al., 2018; Clutterbuck, 2013), specifically in the context of business, is the most applicable literature to the work of a TA TC. In his thesis, Juvonen further suggests (2014, p. 64) that TA Team coaches (TCs) are a cross between the business coach and the life coach as they "help the team entrepreneurs to learn and develop".

The practitioners own personal philosophy and inform their approach to coaching within their discipline. Cox et al. (2018) explain that team coaching is primarily linked to coaches who consider their approach to be cognitive behavioural (which emphasizes the importance of identifying realistic goals and facilitates self-awareness) and developmental (learning about developmental trajectories allows coaches to be better equipped to understand the coachee).

Beyond taxonomies and approaches, other authors, such as Brown and Grant (2010), Clutterbuck (2013), Carter and Hawkins (2013), O'Connor and Cavanagh (2017) and Thornton (2016), have integrated theoretical perspectives and empirical findings from practice to create conceptual frameworks for team coaching practice and all of which helps when undertaking TCg.

The coaching styles continuum (CIPD, 2008) describes the balance that the TC needs to achieve in terms of adopting a push style (more directive, where

DOI: 10.4324/9781003163176-2

the work is done by the coach) or a pull style (non-directive, where the work is done by the learner). Within that spectrum, the TC may adopt different attitudes that go from instructing, suggesting ideas and tips, to asking questions to support the team find solutions, listening, reflecting and reframing.

International Coaching Federation (ICF, 2019) define a number of core competences to understand the skills and approaches used within the coaching profession, these can be used as a professional bedrock for TCg. These include setting the foundation, co-creating the relationship, communicating effectively and facilitating learning and results.

TA TCg specific sources focus on the teampreneur (Tosey et al., 2015; Fowle & Jussila, 2016) and the TA tools rather than on what the TC does (Partanen, 2012; Heikkinen, 2003; Leinonen et al., 2004; Pöysä-Tarhonen et al., 2010). However, the qualities of a TA TC (Partus, 2012) are reflected in the TC's character, which includes elements such as the use of his/her personality, the diversity of the team, keeping one's word, giving feedback and space, or having social skills.

Through the diverse and divergent literature, although an exact definition of TA TCg cannot be found, what does emerge is that at its heart, the TC supports a learning process that endeavours to improve the collective capability and performance of the team (as a system), focuses on the team's shared goals, and uses coaching techniques such as interventions, reflection, awareness, motivation for change and trust building. It implies collaborative action, positive organizational behaviour, communication, and cohesion. It also employs common coaching principles, such as contracting, listening, questioning, observing, giving feedback, exploring actions, or motivating.

Research Methodology

This research uses an embedded multiple case study as a research strategy, as it investigates the phenomenon in a real-life context (Yin, 2003; Saunders, 2009) and analyses different practices in different institutions in the UK. The research is cross-sectional in nature, due to the time limitation for this project. Snowballing was used to access participants, which turned into a non-probability purposive sample (Saunders, 2009, p. 233).

The four sites selected were the University of the West of England Bristol (TA programme launched in 2013), Northumbria University in Newcastle (TA programme launched in 2013), Falmouth University in Cornwall (TA programme launched in 2014), and Bishop Grosseteste University in Lincoln (TA programme launched in 2015). These four institutions were the early adopters, therefore the longest practicing locations for this specific type of pedagogy. Three institutions responded and made up the final group to take part in the research.

Data collection was done in accordance with British Educational Research Association (BERA, 2018) and UWE ethical guidelines, and is based on document analysis, face-to-face interviews and observations. Six interviews were conducted of programme leaders (PLs) and/or team coaches (TCs) from different institutions in the UK, and three observations were conducted in TS of different level teampreneurs (years 1, 2, and 3) one year in each institution.

Findings and Discussion

Main Differences between Programmes

In terms of the modular structure of the programmes analysed at this time, two of the institutions have adopted the TA 3-strand structure (venture, team, and individual strands) for modules. Some of the modules have variations in duration or number of credits but they all cover very similar topics and are all tested and adapted in accordance with staff and TE feedback.

Although all institutions adopt similar assessments (ranging from formal academic essays and business reports to live projects undertaken with real businesses), there are several differences in the forms of assessment used. Most notably, at TAH2 all assessment is undertaken by the TC, whereas at TAH3, this work is shared by the TC and respective module leaders. One more noticeable difference is the volume of assignments, which is higher on TAH3 modules compared to TAH2 handbooks. However, this may be influenced by the shared workload with the module leaders and TCs at TAH3 versus the TAH2 coaches undertaking all marking.

In terms of the size and functioning of the team companies, all TEs work in team companies and have regular TS. However, the size of the teams varies tremendously, from a minimum of 3 to 20, the most common range being between 8 and 14 members. The structure (internal leadership adopted) and subject also vary according to the year of the team company and the interests of the members as does the importance of contracting and TS plans. These factors appear to influence the productivity of the teams and also their ability to deal with issues that arise and ability to clarify how to proceed. Both TCs and team companies use a variety of communication channels, official (Blackboard, Pebble Pad, university email) and alternative (Facebook, Slack, WhatsApp).

Other observations can be made, for example, the introduction of furniture becoming part of the circle during TS (replicating today's common practice in any office environment) and a similar shift towards to more conventional business language terminology.

The use of learning diaries among TCs is common, but some of the hubs rotate TCs and therefore share their coaching diaries:

> *As coaches we have coaching diaries. We have shared diaries, so effectively we both know a bit more about what is going on. We share the coaching across both teams and that's actually worked really well.*
>
> (TAH1B)

TAH2 and TAH3 had handbooks or sections of the handbooks dedicated to the TA terminology and tools (see the Appendix). In those, TAH2 seems to be using terms closely linked to the Finnish heritage of the programme, i.e. the client presentations are called *Birth Givings* the names of the first, second- and third-year students, are given as penguins, seals, and polar bears (Lehtonen, 2013). It remains to be seen how the detail variations will affect the separate hubs and the wider UK TA community as this methodology evolves in the future.

A key difference from the roots of TA common to all institutions is a greater focus on the individual goals, rather than the team goals:

> *One of the most difficult concepts to get my head around, which is something I am still working at and will be for a long, long time, it's the notion of Coaching the Team as a unit.*
>
> (TAH2B)

In the original Finnish model, the team goal of producing profits from team company ventures to fund an around-the-world trip was central. However, when looking at the TA hubs in the UK, there may be as many individual goals as there are TEs and the concept of learning journeys is a different one.

Team Coaching Practices

The role of the TC was articulated in their own unique way by each TC interviewed, however common practices emerged. This section seeks to collate the different practices that the TA UK TC adopt and use.

- Contracting

Some form of agreement regarding how and when the TC worked with their teams existed in all institutions, however not all TCs had an explicit contract or contracting process with their team.

We do not have a contracting process between the coach and the team company but that would be good.

(TAH1B)

- Active listening and questioning

During the training sessions observations, other essential behaviours of the TC are the use of active listening and questioning, this was the case at all the TA Hubs and was employed constantly.

- Intervening

Many of the TCs talk about being inside or outside the circle referring to how directive their coaching is/is not, and how that evolved during the years.

While shadowing the senior coaches, they showed me the model of 1st year, you are within the circle, bringing people together and acting like a bit of a parent figure, 2nd year you take a step back, you want to see more autonomy, giving the team the fishing rod as opposed to the fish, enabling them to do it for themselves.

(TAH1B)

What is quite clear from the interviews is that TCs find intervening and being able not to intervene one of the key functions of their role.

Coaching is a lot of biting your tongue and letting other people do.

(TAH1B)

Clarifying and paraphrasing do however appear to be an important part of the TC's role as seen during observations of TAH2 (year 1 team) where the TC clarified concepts and paraphrased main ideas.

- Rapport building

Building a rapport is an integral part of the team coaching process, regardless of the specific hub and this relationship is fostered and grown, over the duration of the programme:

> *In the first year, I feel that I am the one holding the team together, they are not holding each other together, but as we go through the year the forces of attraction between them get stronger and that's partly my job as well, to enable them to realise that they can be stronger together.*
>
> (TAH2B)

This process is multi-layered and happens at an individual and team level in parallel, which in turn encourages personal and team development:

> *It's about creating an environment where people can flourish and know who they are and be the best they can be.*
>
> (TAH3A)

• Reflection

Year 1 team (TAH2) seemed to be clearly distressed during our observation when they discussed team issues such as absences. The dialogue was open and honest, and the TC was clearly encouraging them to explore issues and reflect on the team's current state. Many TCs would explain how reflection is a crucial element of the TS dialogues:

> *A lot of it is reflecting how you have helped your peers, reflecting on you running a coaching or training session, what value you gave to the individuals, the feedback that was given.*
>
> (TAH1B)

> *Mostly we just let stuff emerge, and if there are any tensions, try and find out what they are coming from, and so look back and reflect on the process of them.*
>
> (TAH2B)

• Facilitating feedback

Through observations it was clear that the TC played an important role in facilitating feedback. For instance, in TAH1 (year 2 team) the TEs presented their projects and obtained feedback from their peers in a quite relaxed and jovial atmosphere:

> *Pitching their business to other people or they are talking through their ideas or they are trying to get honest feedback from people.*
>
> (TAH1B)

• Changing hats

During the observations both in TAH1 (year 2 team) and in TAH2 (year 1 team) it was clear that the TCs could easily shift their role between coaching (questioning, clarifying, paraphrasing, active listening, note taking, pointing out things that are missed, etc.) and directive input as an expert, mentor (using personal past experiences to make a point and show empathy) or module leader, always verbally explaining the change of hats. They also acknowledge how their role is directive depending on which year group they are coaching:

> *All our coaches are also academics, and I am not sure if that is going to stay like that but that has been a deliberate decision and we try and keep the module team pretty tight so that everybody is doing as much as possible of this programme . . . we are in front of different cohorts on the programme wearing different hats. So, I have got three modules as well as being a coach for the First year.*
>
> (TAH1A)

> *The Team Coaches do the marking.*
>
> (TAH2A)

> *In that 1st year I am with the Team, I am really in that centre, I am really helping them and signposting them when it comes to, what is your shared vision? What is your mission? How are you going to contract that you are going to work together and ground rules? You know, those really basic things that are about the TE ethos and the TE way of being and establishing habits. Habits, habits, habits!*
>
> (TAH3B)

TC Training and Coaching Support

Observing the profiles of the participants, the variables that become apparent are the differences and similarities of their professional and educational backgrounds and the number of years of association and participation in the TA course.

It immediately becomes apparent that all the participants have a prevalence of higher levels of education, PhD and masters, or MBAs while others have a wide variety of experience in the private sector. There is also a balanced division between those who have owned and run their own business and those who have operated within organizations. Many TCs emphasized the idea that working on these programmes also helps them within their own businesses:

> *I cannot be around other entrepreneurial people and not be energised. I don't wear a different hat when I am running one of my businesses to when I am working at the University. I think that my mentality has probably changed from seeing other brilliant people on this course.*
>
> (TAH1B)

Most participants have attended the Team Mastery (TM) training programme (Anon, 2021), there being very few, if any, courses nationwide that offer this specific type of training and qualification around TA (beyond ILM level 7 or other equivalent courses). However, there are contrasting opinions about how effective that training is for their team coaching practice:

> *So, I think we're going to look at that, because TM doesn't train you as a coach. And if we are going to onboard people without any Coaching experience, we are going to need to do something.*
>
> (TAH1A)

> *I definitely feel that when I did my Team Mastery, the question was, is this a cult? Are we developing culturally or are we developing a cult? Is this some sort of weird alternative thing.*
>
> (TAH3A)

These comments seem to have a somewhat uncertain view of the effectiveness of the TM programme, in terms of the mechanical application of specific skills, techniques, or frameworks. While the next quote seems to argue there is a more holistic, or thematic value to attending the TM programme:

> *Team Academy is about; what don't you know? Let's find out! Let's go there! Let's get muddy! But it is a shame (not to do the Team Mastery programme), because it's an experience in itself, and I would push for it if I were you.*
>
> (TAH2B)

There are both international and UK versions of the Team Mastery programme. The participants in this research were part of the 2nd and 3rd cohorts who completed the TA UK TM program, in 2014/2015. The current UK programme continues to develop and as it starts with its 9th cohort, incorporates coaching training as part of the delivery, and includes interviews and an induction process that allows the participants to have a clearer understanding of the content and course, so they are able to opt out.

In terms of coaches' coaching development and review, there are differences in the way TCs have or do not have team coaching supervision to create a shared understanding around team coaching best practice:

There's some really good coaching expertise within the Faculty so one friend who does that, offered to run some sessions for us but it's not traditional coaching supervision because it's in a group and you don't get the confidentiality, etc. A colleague was doing team coaching on us, and we were using it as a sort of supervision session, but it didn't work because we ended up talking about operational stuff and it's not confidential.

(TAH1A)

We don't actually have coaching supervision, and that's the really interesting thing, because I think that's something that across the Team Academy network, we are trying to look at developing.

(TAH2A)

We have one to one supervision, year/level supervision (among coaches from the same year) and then the whole team coaching team together.

(TAH3A)

For us to maintain the role of a Team Coach, and for it not to fall back into a classic mentoring or lecturing role, using the theory that is out there, around coaching and what is development for coaching, what is best practice for coaches, supervision is the obvious thing to hook on to ... I see it as a fundamental part of our programme, not just with the supervisors but with peer supervision.

(TAH3B)

All hubs use observations to give feedback to TCs around their practice, but some do it more systematically than others:

We try and discuss the observation contract or any observation beforehand to know whether the person is actually going to be sitting in the circle or not, if there are any specific areas for feedback, and then try and give that feedback afterwards and that feedback can then be brought into supervision.

(TAH3B)

Regardless of the differing perspectives, there is acknowledgement of a clear need for a common basis of understanding and approach, especially when new to the field of TA coaching. Even though not all TCs have done TM programmes, they all engage and *learn by doing* about the TA methodology while they coach their teams and get support from other more experienced TCs (with supervision, etc.) to absorb and integrate that knowledge.

All TCs had a certain attitude towards learning and reflecting about their team coaching role and all of them support their team entrepreneurs not only through their coaching skills but also with the skills, competences and knowledge they bring with them due to their different backgrounds.

Conclusion

The programmes analysed are relatively young within TA internationally. Some programmes are very similar to the original Finnish model, in terms of the terminology used, activities undertaken and general character, while others have changed the terminology. As far as TA methods and tools are concerned however, the core principles remain very similar.

The greatest divergence comes when considering coaching activities taking place in TS. There are clear differences across years in terms of how the TC interacts and intervenes and which approach he/she takes. Another difference links to the details and attention given to the planning of the TS. Only one of the hubs used written plans that are prepared by the teampreneurs prior to the session and communicated to the TC.

The differing use of contracting between the hubs (in addition to the use of the Learning Contract tool (Cunningham, 1999) means that some TCs have a more explicit agreement, in writing, with the team company in relation to how they will work together, roles, responsibilities, and expectations. As contracting is a common practice in other coaching fields, this could be a practice that hubs could adopt to create a dynamic of co-creation and stakeholdership that increases trust and bonding between the team and the TC. It could also be a feature that aligns some hubs more closely with professional coaching approaches.

Regarding TC support structures and training, the most apparent difference was the variation and levels of TC supervision. This was applied with a formal structure, in only one of the hubs (the hub with the largest number of TCs). This mirrored the departure from TM training structures to more internal training that is being adopted across all of the programmes as they mature and develop.

Through the examination of approaches adopted by the UK hubs, this research has found clear evidence that the three UK institutions involved have taken the TA methodology and begun to embrace it and further adapt it to fit a different backdrop in terms of culture, HE structures and cohort demands. There is a clear link that can be followed back to TA roots and ethos in all institutions. The differences identified therefore do not indicate a deviation from the foundations of TA or its underpinning pedagogical philosophy. They highlight the innovative use of the TA methodology by the programme teams themselves when implementing the TA approach, making it fit for purpose as a mechanism of experiential learning like nothing seen before at this programmatic scale in the UK HE sector.

This research provides an important snapshot of how TA UK programmes have integrated the methodology in terms of structure, delivery, and staff support. This will no doubt continue to change and adapt in line with the ethos of the TA methodology itself. Similarly, the full impact of the methodology on the HE sector, not only on business programmes but also in other disciplines, is yet to be fully seen.

The HE sector needs to adapt to an ever faster changing environment if it wants to produce students that are enterprising, ready and able to operate in an interconnected world. The TA methods have a positive contribution to make adding real value to the life of the students and coaches that adopt the TA pedagogy.

References

Anon. (2021). *Applications open for Team Mastery 2021*. Akatemia CIC. https://akatemia.org.uk/applications-process-for-teammastery-9-now-open/

BERA. (2018). *British Educational Research Associations' ethical guidelines for educational research*. Retrieved 4 April 2018 from https://www.bera.ac.uk/publication/ethical-guidelines-for-educational-research-2018-online.

Brown, S. W., & Grant, A. M. (2010). From GROW to GROUP: Theoretical issues and a practical model for group coaching in organisations. *Coaching: An International Journal of Theory, Research and Practice, 3*(1), 30–45. https://doi.org/10.1080/17521880903559697

Carter, A., & Hawkins, P. (2013). Team coaching. Team Coaching. In J. Passmore, D.B. Peterson, & T. Freire (Eds.), *The Wiley Blackwell Handbook of the Psychology of Coaching and Mentoring* (pp.175-194). Oxford: Wiley-Blackwell. https://doi.org/10.1002/9781118326459.ch10

Chartered Institute of Personnel and Development (CIPD). (2008). *Coaching and buying coaching services*. www.portfolio-info.co.uk/files/file/CIPD%20 coaching_buying_services.pdf

Clutterbuck, D. (2013). Time to focus coaching on the team. *Industrial and Commercial Training, 44*, 18–22. https://doi.org/10.1108/00197851311296665

Cox, E., Bachkirova, T., & Clutterbuck, D. (Eds.). (2018). *The complete handbook of coaching* (3rd ed.). London: SAGE Publications Ltd.

Cunningham, I. (1999). *The wisdom of strategic learning: The self managed learning solution* (2nd ed.). Aldershot: Gower. https://doi.org/10.4324/9781315551449-9

Fowle, M., & Jussila, N. (2016). The adoption of a Finnish learning model in the UK. 11th *European conference on innovation and entrepreneurship*, 15-16 September 2016, Jyvaskyla, Finland.

Garvey, B., Stokes, P., & Megginson, D. (2017). *Coaching and mentoring: Theory and practice* (3rd ed.). London: SAGE. https://doi.org/10.1177/0974173920100214

Hawkins, P. (2017). *Leadership team coaching: Developing collective transformational leadership* (3rd ed.). London: Kogan Page. https://doi.org/10.1111/peps.12006_5

Heikkinen, H. (2003). Team Academy: A story of a school that learns. *Development and Learning in Organizations: An International Journal, 17*(1), 7–9. https://doi.org/10.1108/13697230310458495

ICF.(2019). *ICF core competencies—UK ICF*.https://doi.org/10.1007/springerreference_ 223987

Juvonen, P. (2014). Learning information technology business in a changing industry landscape. Introducing team entrepreneurship in renewing bachelor education in information [thesis for the degree of doctor of science (Technology), Lappeenranta University of Technology, Lappeenranta, Finland].*Acta Universitatis Lappeenrantaensis*. Available from https://lutpub.lut.fi/bitstream/handle/10024/ 102204/Pasi%20Juvonen%20A4%2021%2011%20.pdf?sequence=2& isAllowed=y.

Lehtonen, T. (2013). *Team Academy—How to grow into a teampreneur. Tiimiakatemia*. Jyväskylä: JAMK University of Applied Sciences.

Leinonen, N., Partanen, J., & Palviainen, P. (2004). *The Team Academy: A true story of a community that learns by doing*. Jyväskylä: PS-kustannus.

Lyle, J., & Cushion, C. (2016). *Sports coaching: Professionalisation and practice* (2nd ed.). Edinburgh: Churchill Livingstone.

Neenan, M., & Dryden, W. (2013). *Life coaching: A cognitive behavioural approach*. London: Routledge. https://doi.org/10.4324/9780203362853.

O'Connor, S., & Cavanagh, M. (2017). Group and team coaching. In T. Bachkirova, G. Spence, & D. Drake (Eds.), *The SAGE handbook of coaching* (pp. 486–504). Sage Publications, Inc. Partanen, J. (2012). *The team coach's best tools*. Jyväskylä: Partus.

Partus. (2012). *Creation of team coach's character. Prematerials* [Power Point slides] Tiimi Mestari, Partus.

Pöysä-Tarhonen, J., Toivanen, H., Elen, J., Tarhonen, P., Hirvanen, M., & Kymäläinen, T. (2010). Emerging student team companies: Studying the quality of dialogue and collaborative learning. In Finpin Conference, Innovation and Entrepreneurship in Universities, Joensuu University, Finland.

Saunders, M., Lewis, P., & Thornhill, A. (2009). *Research methods for business students* (5th ed.). Harlow: Pearson Education Limited.

Thornton, C. (2016). *Group and team coaching: The secret life of groups*. London: Routledge. https://doi.org/10.4324/9781315684956

Tosey, P., Dhaliwal, S., & Hassinen, J. (2015). The Finnish Team Academy model: Implications for management education. *Management Learning, 46*(2), 175–194. https://doi.org/10.1177/1350507613498334

Yates, J. (2013). *The career coaching handbook*. London: Routledge. https://doi.org/10.4324/9781315867366

Yin, R. (2003). *Case study research and applications* (3rd ed.). Thousand Oaks, CA: Sage Publications, pp. 5–6, 22–27, 38–55. https://doi.org/10.1111/j.1540-4781.2011.01212_17.x

Apendix

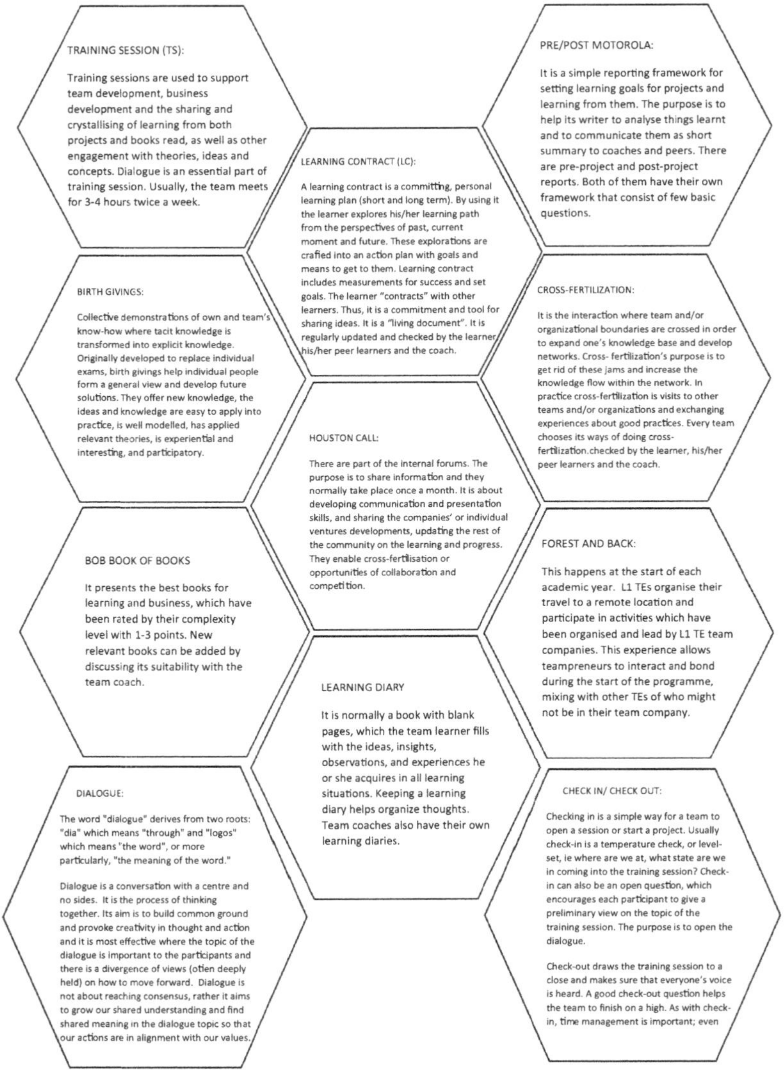

TRAINING SESSION (TS):

Training sessions are used to support team development, business development and the sharing and crystallising of learning from both projects and books read, as well as other engagement with theories, ideas and concepts. Dialogue is an essential part of training session. Usually, the team meets for 3-4 hours twice a week.

BIRTH GIVINGS:

Collective demonstrations of own and team's know-how where tacit knowledge is transformed into explicit knowledge. Originally developed to replace individual exams, birth givings help individual people form a general view and develop future solutions. They offer new knowledge, the ideas and knowledge are easy to apply into practice, is well modelled, has applied relevant theories, is experiential and interesting, and participatory.

BOB BOOK OF BOOKS

It presents the best books for learning and business, which have been rated by their complexity level with 1-3 points. New relevant books can be added by discussing its suitability with the team coach.

DIALOGUE:

The word "dialogue" derives from two roots: "dia" which means "through" and "logos" which means "the word", or more particularly, "the meaning of the word."

Dialogue is a conversation with a centre and no sides. It is the process of thinking together. Its aim is to build common ground and provoke creativity in thought and action and it is most effective where the topic of the dialogue is important to the participants and there is a divergence of views (often deeply held) on how to move forward. Dialogue is not about reaching consensus, rather it aims to grow our shared understanding and find shared meaning in the dialogue topic so that our actions are in alignment with our values.

LEARNING CONTRACT (LC):

A learning contract is a committing, personal learning plan (short and long term). By using it the learner explores his/her learning path from the perspectives of past, current moment and future. These explorations are crafied into an action plan with goals and means to get to them. Learning contract includes measurements for success and set goals. The learner "contracts" with other learners. Thus, it is a commitment and tool for sharing ideas. It is a "living document". It is regularly updated and checked by the learner, his/her peer learners and the coach.

HOUSTON CALL:

There are part of the internal forums. The purpose is to share information and they normally take place once a month. It is about developing communication and presentation skills, and sharing the companies' or individual ventures developments, updating the rest of the community on the learning and progress. They enable cross-fertlisation or opportunities of collaboration and competition.

LEARNING DIARY

It is normally a book with blank pages, which the team learner fills with the ideas, insights, observations, and experiences he or she acquires in all learning situations. Keeping a learning diary helps organize thoughts. Team coaches also have their own learning diaries.

PRE/POST MOTOROLA:

It is a simple reporting framework for setting learning goals for projects and learning from them. The purpose is to help its writer to analyse things learnt and to communicate them as short summary to coaches and peers. There are pre-project and post-project reports. Both of them have their own framework that consist of few basic questions.

CROSS-FERTILIZATION:

It is the interaction where team and/or organizational boundaries are crossed in order to expand one's knowledge base and develop networks. Cross- fertilization's purpose is to get rid of these jams and increase the knowledge flow within the network. In practice cross-fertilization is visits to other teams and/or organizations and exchanging experiences about good practices. Every team chooses its ways of doing cross-fertilization.checked by the learner, his/her peer learners and the coach.

FOREST AND BACK:

This happens at the start of each academic year. L1 TEs organise their travel to a remote location and participate in activities which have been organised and lead by L1 TE team companies. This experience allows teampreneurs to interact and bond during the start of the programme, mixing with other TEs of who might not be in their team company.

CHECK IN/ CHECK OUT:

Checking in is a simple way for a team to open a session or start a project. Usually check-in is a temperature check, or level-set, ie where are we at, what state are we in coming into the training session? Check-in can also be an open question, which encourages each participant to give a preliminary view on the topic of the training session. The purpose is to open the dialogue.

Check-out draws the training session to a close and makes sure that everyone's voice is heard. A good check-out question helps the team to finish on a high. As with check-in, time management is important; even

Figure A1. TA tools and terms simplified

Source: Authors' own

2 A Hybrid Model in Tourism Postgraduate Education – A Learning Journey

Georgiana Els

The Character

"You have brains in your head. You have feet in your shoes. You can steer yourself any direction you choose (. . .) So be sure when you step. Step with care and great tact and remember that Life's a Great Balancing Act" (Seuss, 1990).

I have been introduced to team learning and Team Academy (TA) methods in the steep paths of the Himalayas in May 2013 while attending the first walking conference on social entrepreneurship in tourism. While discussing the future of education and debating on the values that should govern the tourism world, the novel TA approach came to strengthen my belief that education and, mainly, tourism education needs reshaping. Tourism education is in need of a fundamental change that is not incremental by adjusting or adding new programmes, changing the names of modules in order to make it timely and catchy and moving to blended or online learning, but changing the nature of what is taught and how is taught (Sheldon et al., 2014). This was the moment when a seed was planted, the beginning of a long journey which I know started in Nepal, in a place of great spiritual significance, but I did not know where and how it would end.

My coaching journey started out of a personal desire for self-discovery, growing and learning. I have joined the Team Mastery programme without fully understanding what I am embarking on, but having an ardour for self-awareness, mind stretching, and new challenges. As *a journey of a thousand miles begins with a single step* (Lao Tzu, n.d.), my first step started with a birth-giving in the village of Bumburi, Nepal, where the founder of TA Brazil coached a team of tourism academics.

My role as a parent, educator, tourism professional, and consultant was reshaped in 2017 by joining the Mastery Programme and entering the TA international community. I was able to gain personal experience through learning by doing, experiencing the triangle of team entrepreneurship:

DOI: 10.4324/9781003163176-3

leader-learner-coach, reflecting on the experiences, critically evaluating methods and tools (e.g. business simulations, action learning) and contributing to building the TA international community. The change in paradigm of learning makes TA a life's journey that brings me closer to Gandhi's thoughts and the personal belief that if we could change ourselves, the tendencies in the world would also change.

The Setting

Since the early 90s there has been a constant growth in entrepreneurship education taught in universities, and mainly in business schools. The growth is related to modules and programmes in entrepreneurship, growing research in the field and research centres, think tanks and incubators and strengthening university-business collaborations. Likewise, when we discuss the area of tourism education there is a palette of programmes, courses, and modules offered in entrepreneurship. In an evaluation of teaching methods of entrepreneurship across tourism and hospitality university programmes, Ahmad et al. (2018) note that while most frequent techniques remain traditional, no single method alone seems to be appropriate to achieve course objectives.

The Team Academy (*Tiimiakatemia* in Finnish) philosophy advanced by Johannes Partanen started in 1993 and has spread across the World to become a phenomenon of team learning. Its ability to multiply and spread rapidly made it reach new mediums and like any living organism it has grown and evolved. There is not a single TA model anymore; we are witnessing a model in practice that has taken the shapes and forms of the local landscapes.

The book you are holding describes how TA model of entrepreneurial education has evolved and moulded in diverse settings and contexts. And the proposed chapter tells the story of a newly developed postgraduate programme in International Tourism Management (MSc ITM) and its integrated coaching module TOU9166M Personal Professional Development (PPD) which has been developed on the basis of TA methodologies. The programme is unique and timely making the point of discussion due to its innovative approach: (1) implementing parts of TA philosophy and methodologies in a (2) master programme in (3) tourism education with the aim of (4) developing an entrepreneurial/intrapreneurial mind in young adults.

The Conflict

When embarking on the journey of the reshaped programme, I had a Socratic dialogue with myself, trying to ask the right questions at the right time. What do I want to see happening? Why does it need to happen? What would it mean to me? What would it mean to my students? In this way, I was trying to get closer to the extent in which TA was replicable in other contexts and most importantly, its applicability in the context of postgraduate tourism education. If I had to personify the programme, what beast I would want it to be?

Instead of creating another version of an already existing tourism programme, the new model aimed at placing students at the core by combining TA philosophy with TEFI's (Tourism Education Futures Initiative) values and principles recognizing that today's students are tomorrow's industry, government and third sector and that the future of tourism rests with them (Dredge et al., 2015). Which brings me to the obvious questions – What is the future of tourism education?

The Plot

In an era where higher education (HE) is driven by metrics and TEF, REF and KEF (Teaching Excellence Framework, Research Excellence Framework and Knowledge Exchange Framework) are setting the rules of the game, there is a real need for novel methods and models. Ahmad et al. (2018) suggest the introduction of innovative approaches, by promoting student-led activities in the classroom to stimulate engagement and create an optimal medium for the learning process while emphasizing the underlying theories. In such model, the significance of networked teams is crucial, and the model should be transparent, digitally aligned, scalable, and adaptable (Deloitte, 2016).

With the MSc International Tourism Management programme and core coaching module that underpins it, a heutagogical learning environment was created where students take the ownership of their learning and careers by mainly addressing (1) new insights into teaching, learning, and research; (2) individual needs in a team setting and, thus, improving student attainment; and (3) students equipped for high levels of uncertainty and a fast-changing environment.

A retrospective reflection on the programme first year of running was definitely on the cards at the end of its first cycle, however what came unexpectedly were the events of 2020 that have been disruptive, raised extremely high levels of unpredictability and affected tourism industry in an unprecedented way globally. Then the question arises: Could the black swan of 2020 be the event that reshapes our systems and organizations? In order to succeed in a volatile environment, our students have to be equipped with the necessary skills to lead in a confident knowledgeable manner by providing cross-functional coaching and development with a focus on team dynamics to drive a socially and environmentally responsible change (Deloitte, 2016).

Cross-pollination of beliefs and ideas during the process of learning and development is a main factor in the success of a module and the programme overall. As portraited by Senge et al. (2012, p. 162), a learning classroom means not only that students are able to learn, but that they can learn in a range of ways and acquire noteworthy skills and competences no matter their age, background, or previous experiences. In such a learning environment, students understand that part of their purpose is making sure every member of the team succeeds. As Deloitte highlights (2016, p. 11), *connected teams are smarter than the individuals that comprise them* and in order to succeed in today's ever-changing business climate, organizations should share the risks and exploit the collaborative environment. The MSc ITM programme was designed in close collaboration to industry to prepare students for a dynamic work environment. The programme is formed around three leading principles.

Firstly, on the idea of 'student as producer' (Neary, 2010), which promotes the involvement and engagement of students in the design, delivery, and assessment of modules and programmes.

Secondly, on the five TEFI values (Dredge et al., 2015, p. 341):

1) Stewardship – Exercising an ethic of care by upholding principles associated with sustainability, responsibility, and service to the community;
2) Knowledge – Developing critical thinking, innovation, creativity, and networking and appreciating different sources and types of knowledge about tourism;
3) Professionalism – Aspiring to the highest standards of professional practice underpinned by leadership, practicality, services, relevance, timeliness, reflexivity, teamwork, and partnerships;
4) Ethics – Engaging in good action and decision-making, underpinned by honesty, fairness, transparency, and authentic dialogue; and
5) Mutual respect – Embracing a humanistic approach to tourism, including a respect for diversity, inclusion, equity, humility, and collaboration

And thirdly on the principles of Team Academy:

6) Learning means developing personal, behavioural, and hard skills;
7) Learning requires taking real responsibility for real businesses; and
8) Learning takes place at an individual, team, and community level

The MSc ITM programme developed at University of Lincoln (UoL) aims to develop in students the skills, knowledge, and personal qualities required to develop and flourish in a tourism organization and/or business start-up.

The coaching module (PPD) is designed around the TA principles and aims at fostering a postgraduate community where flexibility, creativity, and innovation are key. Through the course of the module, students are setting individual goals by developing a "Learning Contract" and are assessed according to individual progress and development. Thus, they become self-directed and more self-evaluative. Students are coached through the degree, the role of the coach/coaches being to facilitate students' abilities to self-manage and take responsibility of their own learning and development. The coaches provide advice in a non-directive manner in a shared environment where learners are participants in the process: *I feel being cared for as a person not just a student. The decisions made in the creation of the module feel like they have been made with great care to the good of the students* (student enrolled on the programme, Interview 2020).

In an analysis of teaching methods of entrepreneurship in tourism programmes, Ahmad et al. (2018) outline an overview of teaching methods by suggesting a mixed approach between traditional and more innovative ones. The teaching and learning methods can be classified as:

- Passive methods: lectures, case studies, business plan.
- Active methods: business simulation games, guest speakers, business visits and field trips.
- Experiential methods: consultancy project, project-based learning, counselling/mentoring practical training and working with entrepreneurs, start your own business.

Tourism education is known for graduate students who have a strong ground for innovation and entrepreneurship at the subjective cognitive level, and enthusiasm to engage in innovation and entrepreneurship is at a medium high level, however these students are not confident in their abilities to demonstrate innovation and entrepreneurship and thus universities should strengthen their provision in the areas (Chen & Zhang, 2020).

The MSc ITM programme adopts a refreshing approach to assessment and feedback, aiming to create an environment where assessment is regarded as a learning event where students have access to their own data, are aware of where they stand, what needs improving and that they should take responsibility of their own learning. Assessment as learning is embedded within the modules and as the tutors provide feedback, students are engaged in learning about how to improve. Students demonstrated capability in setting their own goals and oversee their progress. In this way, students become self-directed and more self-evaluative.

> *By being coached in an interaction way and assessed through a variety of methods, the course has not only encouraged further learning and development but provided a platform and network system for a thriving future career in the tourism industry.*
>
>   (Student enrolled on the programme, Interview 2020)

The Team Academy curriculum is represented graphically through the Rocket Model, which is the model in *Tiimiakatemia*, being present on the wall of every team crib. The Rocket model represents the learning journey or the stages of development for each of the team companies. It resembles a space rocket and growth of team companies happens upwards from the bottom. The base represents the engine and is formed of three processes: The Process of Individual Learning, The Process of Team Learning, and the Process of Team-Company Learning. The 14 processes of the model are interrelated and without individual learning efforts, the other processes will not develop either. The TA Rocket Model is detailed by Partanen (2016, pp. 12–13) in what is the most popular teampreneurs' book *The Team Coach's Best Tools*.

While the Rocket Model represents a good tool for the MSc ITM programme and integrated coaching model, it was not possible to replicate it as the aim of our postgraduate tourism programme is not set on the creation and development of the team company. However, certain elements of the model and mainly the dynamics of individual-team learning were of utmost importance. Figure 2.1 features my reinterpretation of the Rocket Model to highlight the structure and balance of individual/team/business assessments in the postgraduate programme developed.

The Rocket Model for Assessment Mapping developed for MSc International Tourism Management at University of Lincoln portrays the structure of the programme and its assessment mapping. The model is made up of 7 vertical lines, 8 horizontal levels, and 16 examples of individual and team assessments. The core vertical line represents the modules offered in the degree where knowledge is accumulated through more 'traditional' methods; the right side is represented by students' individual learning and assessments while the left represents the process of team learning and team assessments. The four dotted lines underpin the programme as they are present in multiple shapes and forms and happen through the duration of the programme: Digital Capabilities, Professional Practice Mentoring, Stewardship and The Team Coaching Process. At the end of their first year of studies, students have the option of a year in industry. Fundamentally, the programme aims to achieve a good balance between individual and team learning by enabling the coaching and mentorship processes.

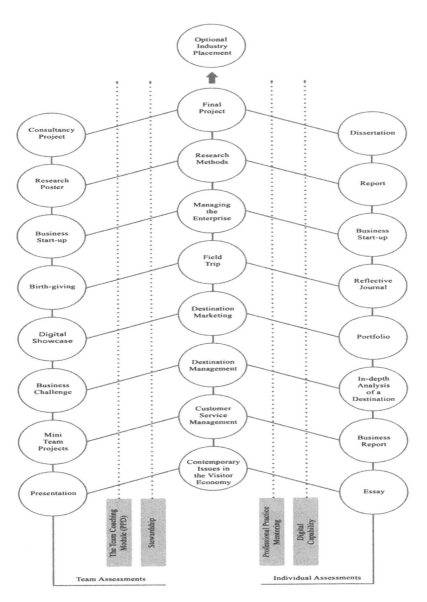

Figure 2.1 Model for Assessment Mapping

Source: Author's own

Resolution – Looking Back and Moving Forward

My first 'deep' reflection on my coaching style and practice was done at the end of the Team Mastery programme when I wrote my coaching philosophy, a viewpoint which has grown since with my practice. The first principles to be applied in my coaching practice came from parenthood. Kohn's (2006, p. 119) principles of unconditional parenting worked in my coaching relation with my students: (1) be reflective; (2) reconsider your requests; (3) keep your eye on the long-term goals; (4) put the relationship first; (5) change how you see, not just how you act; (6) respect; (7) be authentic; (8) talk less, ask more; (9) keep their age in mind; (10) attribute to students the best possible motive consistent with the facts; (11) don't stick to No's unnecessarily; (12) don't be rigid; and (13) don't be in a hurry. Unconditional parenting and unconditional student coaching are similar on most levels and I believe that both are deeply rooted in our childhood and relation to the family and cultural system. A lot of work and understanding need to happen at a personal level in order to reach a coaching maturity.

A retrospective view is definitely needed as the programme progresses from babyhood to toddlerhood. What is the learning from the first year and how can it be applied? For the past year and a half, reflections have been somehow part of my weekly routine and my students have given me the confidence that the model created (Figure 2.1) grows with me or better should I say that I grow with it?

The Good, the Bad, and the Ugly

My experience from joining the TA programme to applying the methodology in a different setting makes my journey unique and timely. Unique as the programme has been applied at postgraduate level outside of its core TA satellites in the UK in a visitor economy context. And timely, as I see the model being similarly replicated in other programmes and degrees. The aim is to take my learnings further and hopefully what *I have learned* will help inspire other academics, team coaches, teampreneurs, and students to take team learning to future horizons.

The newly developed programme and its integrated coaching module (PPD) gathered positive responses from students, external examiners, other staff, and business partners. As an integrated part, the PPD module underpins the programme by coaching and mentoring students from the moment they enrol by the time they finish their degree. The excellent feedback meant an extension to other postgraduate degrees such as Events Management, International Hospitality Management, and Sports Business Management, with discussions to further extend across several disciplines (e.g., marketing, heritage). While being proud of the model and enjoying its development, *I have learned* that scaling up needs to be gradual as there are several aspects identified in the first year of running it that need starting, refining, or perfecting as detailed in the points below.

In a hybrid programme where teaching still takes the majority of the workload, I find it a real challenge to be able to switch from teaching to coaching sometimes just in as little as ten minutes. I am still learning and improving techniques to switch my brain from a teaching mode to a coaching mode in a very short time span. *I have learned* that small steps can make a huge difference when you build it up in your daily routine and train your brain.

One of the challenges encountered in my first year of coaching was coaching alone, not being able to share meaningful conversation with a fellow coach. Those corridor discussions and meaningful dialogues after an intense coaching session were missing and made me feel hesitant and doubtful at times. The exploration of innovative methods felt slower as I was double questioning my actions and practice. However, this step was somehow overcome as *I have learned* to connect to core TA programmes and starting to enable those conversations. A morning coffee catch-up with a fellow coach is something to look forward to and provides a boost of energy by reassuring you are on the right path and *if not*, new paths need exploring anyhow. The connection with other coaches inevitably led to meaningful collaborations at teampreneurs/student level—I would say that the most genuine reflections and constructive feedback came after joint sessions as students understood why we have to unlearn in order to learn and that we are part of a bigger community to which they also belong.

The first cohort of students had a fantastic engagement with the programme and mainly with the tools and methods used in the coaching sessions. This meant that by the end of term two, some of the students were ready to embark in external collaborations with private and public organizations and thus, play an active role in the local community. The students involved had the opportunity to gain new skills and work on live projects that contributed to the university's civic mission. The benefits of the collaborations were trifold: staff—students—local community. *I have learned* to continuously think of how the model can be used and adapted to suit various needs and learners. The downsize was that some of the projects had to be stopped due to the outbreak of COVID-19 and following lockdowns.

The overnight move to online delivery was new to students and academics alike. Data collected at university level shows students responded in various ways to the challenge—some engaged better in the online environment while others struggled with the new way of delivery. In the chaos of the first lockdown, my team of students supported each other and made sure each member of their team strived. The support and collaboration they have demonstrated at an academic and personal level showed the power of their team! *We have all learned* what it means to be equipped for high levels of uncertainty and having to strive in an ever fast-changing climate.

The chapter is an exploration of the author's journey from the first engagement with TA methods to present day by narrating key moments. The focus is the development of a postgraduate programme in tourism which combines several elements underpinned by the Finnish TA philosophy. From how the idea was initiated, to the development and running of the degree, and to lessons learned, the aim is to share what has been done during this time, hoping it will pave the way for the implementation and application of other hybrid models in various disciplines. The novelty and uniqueness of the programme has been discussed by highlighting key elements such as postgraduate experience, tourism education, entrepreneurship, students' skills, assessment, community of learning, and communities of practice. My one-thousand-mile learning journey continues with small steps and this chapter is one of them.

References

Ahmad, S. Z., Bakar, A. R. A., & Ahmad, N. (2018). An evaluation of teaching methods of entrepreneurship in hospitality and tourism programs. *International Journal of Management in Education, 16*(1), 14–25. www.tandfonline.com/doi/abs/10.1080/10963758.2014.998764

Chen, S., & Zhang, M. (2020). Research on cultivation and development of graduate students' innovation and entrepreneurship consciousness. *Higher Education Studies, 10*(2), 45–52. https://doi.org/10.5539/hes.v10n2p45

Deloitte. (2016). *Unlocking the flexible organisation. Organisational design for an uncertain future.* https://www2.deloitte.com/global/en/pages/human-capital/articles/gx-unlocking-the-flexible-organization.html

Dredge, D., Schott, C., Daniele, R., Caton, K., Edelheim, J., & Munar, A. M. (2015). The tourism education futures initiative. *Anatolia, 26*(2), 340–346. https://doi.org/10.1080/13032917.2014.930773

Kohn, A. (2006). *Unconditional parenting.* New York: Atria Paperback.

Neary, M. (2010). Student as producer: A pedagogy for the avant-garde, or how do revolutionary teachers teach? *Learning Exchange, 1*(1). https://studentasproducer.lincoln.ac.uk/files/2014/03/15-72-1-pb-1.pdf

Lao Tzu. (n.d.). *Attributed to Lao-Tzu (c 604—c 531bc), founder of Taoism.* BBC World Service. www.bbc.co.uk/worldservice/learningenglish/movingwords/shortlist/laotzu.shtml

Partanen, J. (2016). *The team coach's best tools.* Jyväskylä: Partus.

Senge, P., Cambron-McCabe, N., Lucas, T., Smith, B., Dutton, J., & Kleiner, A. (2012). *Schools that learn.* London: Nicholas Brealey Publishing.

Seuss, D. R. (1990). *Oh, The Places You'll Go!* New York: Penguin Random House.

Sheldon, P., Fesenmaier, D., & Tribe, J. (2014). The Tourism Education Futures Initiative (TEFI): Activating change in tourism education. In D. Prebezac, C. Schott, & P. Sheldon (Eds.), *The Tourism Education Futures Initiative: Activating change in tourism education* (pp. 14–35). London: Routledge www.tandfonline.com/doi/abs/10.1080/15313220.2011.548728

3   Increasing Human Agency Through Team Learning in Finnish Basic Education

Tuula Koivukangas and Päivi Rimpiläinen

Equal Basic Education

The actions of the *Parasta ennen* (translated as "Best Before") Project in Pohjois Savo are the result of a dream for equality in basic education. Solutions have been sought in 21 primary schools to ensure that every child and young person has the opportunity to acquire skills and knowledge and to be encountered in a positive way. This goal has been achieved through team learning for all of the adults at the schools.

In many ways, Finnish primary schools are undergoing a transition between the old and new operating cultures. How can we respond to increasing needs and the various challenges posed by learning and well-being? How can we ensure the well-being of whole school communities? How can we ensure that equality in basic education is achieved in every school, in every class, and for every child in our rapidly changing world? How can a whole school community learn together?

The *Parasta ennen Project* has been supporting the development of a communal working culture and pedagogy in the participating schools. Actions have been sought that support preventive systemic change and new ways of co-operation with non-educational professionals like those in student welfare services and youth work who work in schools. We begin our actions getting to know the individual circumstances of each school at the grass-roots level. The actors in the project include multi-professional staff of each school. The school staff jointly participated in an experiential learning process according to principles of team learning. School communities have received tailor-made coaching from professionals in team learning, coaching, drama education, and participation.

A model of five main paths was formed to support schools. All 21 schools were involved in a cyclic process of development. The five main paths are as follows:

DOI: 10.4324/9781003163176-4

1. Team coaching: The team coaches coach the school management team five times a year. In turn, the school management team leaders coach their learning teams between the visits of the team coaches. The team coaches encourage the principals of the schools in the learning cycle.
2. Drama training: Drama educators have trained the staff of the schools; they have taught sessions and held parents' evenings, as well as formed their own team, through which they have disseminated skills and knowledge about drama education in schools. The goal of drama education is to support constructive interaction and group processes. Drama educators visited schools five times a year.
3. Coaching sessions for team learning: The school management team have participated in *Tiimiakatemia®* *Kick-Start* for team learning-coaching sessions. Team learning is the all-embracing mindset and the way of acting for the entire project. *Tiimiakatemia®* *Kick-Start—process lasts four months. It includes five coaching days.*
4. Research: The project has generated data at three levels. Researchers from the University of Eastern Finland (UEF) have examined the development of agency in professional communities and classrooms, the progress of management and the learning of individual teachers. Research was implemented in years 2019–2020.
5. Co-creation: A digital tool for co-creation, *Innoduel*, has been used in the project. Principals have practiced participatory approaches using the tool. During the project, principals have received training on how to create opportunities for staff to participate. In addition, they have received training in management communication.

The schools' management teams' objective with this project was to make a change in the development of those schools. This requires individual skills and will to make a change. This type of experience of agency is the basis for systemic chance in communities. Systemic change is understood as the change of ways of action and structures. These kinds of changes create the prerequisites for well-being and humane courses of action in basic education. In team learning process, individual agency increases. The assets that are gained through team learning are the most important resource in communities. A common asset is a resource and prerequisite in facing and resolving complicated problems in schools. For the learning and work of adults at schools to be connected, a structure that facilitates and enables this process is needed. The structure and model of on-the-job learning make it possible for school adults to participate. Participation is one of the prerequisites of commitment. The ways in which adults act in professional communities will inevitably affect the ways in which young people act in similar situations.

On-the-job learning as a goal for the entire community is a new thing in Finnish schools. Traditionally, teachers seek professional training according to their own interests, but a systematic learning that embraces the whole school community, especially through team learning, is not usual. Finnish teachers have great autonomy to plan their teaching within the curriculum. Furthermore, Finnish teachers work very much independently. The emotional skills of the school adults and a safe atmosphere in the learning situations created by the adults are prerequisites for kids learning. To ensure equal opportunities for every child, all the school adults need to learn together and co-operate. Successful change is more likely to be achieved when all the members of the community are involved from the very beginning. Team learning through dialogue and coaching increases the skills and the will to work together in a jointly agreed direction. Increasingly, different ways of co-operation also occur.

Team Learning as a Course of Action in the School Community

The team serves as a tool for individual learning. Team learning can be carried out at each level of the school community. The professional community and the classroom community comprise individuals. Each individual has the same basic needs (feeling of belonging to group, autonomy, and competence), which need to be met to achieve learning. In teams, the individual's intrinsic motivation is awakened, which, in turn, increases their experience of agency and social participation (Norrena, 2019). Each individual's learning forms the basis for team learning, and, eventually, the base for a change of action in their work community/organization. The individual's learning is supported by inspiring them to read and encouraging them to try and experiment with things (for example dialogue circle) in their own work. Knowledge is built through dialogue. During coaching sessions, it is possible to share and reflect upon issues that have arisen from that reading and/or experiments. The team serves as a space for this kind of experiential learning.

The course of action for team learning in professional communities includes in-advance preparation, dialogues, experiments, and reflection. When school adults learn to act according to the mindset of team learning in their own communities, the course of action is inevitably transferred to classrooms. In this so-called parallel process, the phenomena and actions in a group transform to the next level (Haapaniemi & Raina, 2014).

Books, blogs, articles, or podcasts are used as preview material. The meaning of preview learning is to facilitate the dialogue in coaching and deepen the individual's and the team's understanding of the matter at hand. The meaning of in-advance preparation as a part of the learning cycle is significant. It offers the members of the team the opportunity and the time to process information and to form an opinion on the issue. At the same time, it provides a feeling of social participation. There are always individuals in teams who prefer to stay in the background of the dialogue. In-advance preparation and the opportunity to reflect beforehand provide individuals with a feeling of security and the confidence to participate in the dialogue.

According to the mindset of flipped learning, familiarization with a theory in advance renders learning more effectively (Toivola et al., 2020). Team members can connect theory with their everyday life experiences. The learning outcome or solution of a team is constructed through common understanding. The task of the coach is to summarize, review the issues discussed, encourage, reflect, raise questions, and listen.

The teams' coaching sessions are carried out in dialogue circles. The coaches have the important responsibility to create a warm and informal atmosphere between the people sitting in the dialogue circle. In this circle, people are open to and present for each other. Notes are taken using notebooks, and phones and computers are left outside of the dialogue circle, according to the agreement/ground rules of the team. The same structure is followed each time in the coaching sessions. Repetition and consistency build the feeling of security in individuals, in teams, and in the whole work community. Figure 3.1 shows the structure of a coaching session:

Check in

Dialogue
Building shared understanding

Working
Clarifying core matters

Planning
Commencing the planning of work community training

Check out

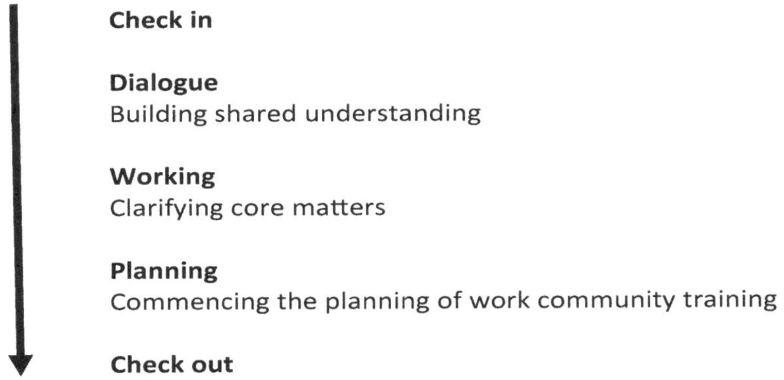

C

Figure 3.1 Structure of a Coaching Session
Source: Author's own

Dialogue is one of the learning goals of a team, and its success requires a great deal of practice in many communities. The four principles of dialogue comprise one important part of the team's agreement. Respecting others, listening, waiting, and speaking out of one's heart are skills that also require training (Isaacs, 1999). At the beginning of the session, the team is often reminded of the principles of dialogue. Through a common understanding, constructed in the dialogue, a common direction becomes clear and readiness to experiment increases.

Experiments are an important part of learning process. It is possible to plan longer or shorter experiments from the learning material to be realized in the working environment. One principal conducted experiments with the school management team in this way: members of the school management team experimented dialogue skills with learning teams and educational staff experimented dialogue skills with their student groups.

One important stage in the process of experiential learning is reflection. In the reflection stage, the success of experiments is discussed, as well as the possibility to adopt those new ways of working. Learning can first be reflected upon individually, but the reflection between team members constructs the shared learning.

Learning in a community occurs by repeating the cycle of on-the-job learning. The learning of the entire community makes progress slowly, yet in a very influential way. In one of the *Tiimiakatemia®️ Kick-Start* team learning-session, a game called *Next Level* was created. That is how a team learning coaching cycle was realized in a playful way. The game is suitable for adults' on-the-job learning as well as for practicing team learning with children and young people.

Multifunctional Team Organization as Structure of *On-the-Job* Learning

In the course of the project, many schools have developed a team organization. This is, permanent learning staff teams have been integrated into the school's structure. These learning teams are coached by team Leaders from the school's management team. The learning teams meet regularly, and they work with their own learning goals and with tasks related to the whole school. In addition, these teams are part of the school's decision-making system. In the structure of a team, it is possible to gain common learning in organization. Creating such a structure requires the school principal and the management team to have the courage and confidence that the structure will bring something good to both the individuals and the community. The traditional culture of individual working might create some opposition to such a team organization in schools. Conversely, in many schools, people are aware that working alone increases cynicism and burnout. The principal and school management team can enable a culture of interaction and communal learning in their school. To outline this demanding entity, principals need to provide support and structures for their own learning. At the municipality and state levels, education providers are part of the system. Policies and structures should also support the integration of principals' work around learning.

The structure of coaching is the same in both learning and management teams. The management team chooses the contents and working methods when working on a development phase for the working community. Training dialogue and supporting the group processes are central to the choice of methods. The feeling of belonging, autonomy, and the feeling that one's skills and knowledge matter are the beginning of motivation and involvement. The point here is the emergence of agency, which might appear as proactive deeds, enthusiasm, and discoveries of new and creative solutions.

There is a delay in learning in the work community compared to the management team. Schools have found different solutions to make this delay shorter, for instance by creating a learning environment where the learners can browse books, borrow them, or go deeper into the development process of a working culture. Repetition of working methods, predictability, and clarity in the coaching sessions of learning teams increase the feeling of safety in the community. When the coaching sessions are connected to everyday life, the delay of learning is shortened. In the coaching sessions of learning teams, each individual is encouraged to have some experiments in their working environment where they apply what they learnt in coaching sessions. The ideas that arise during the experiments are reflected back in the following coaching session. Through on-the-job learning, individuals also acquire the skills to carry out team learning in their own classroom. When adults develop their own skills in dialogue (voicing, listening, respecting, and suspending), her/his skills in guiding learner groups increase also. In schools where teachers are organized in a collective way and learn together, students' learning is organized in a similar way (Haapaniemi & Raina, 2014).

The principal is the one who enables on-the-job learning in the community and guides the school management team together with the vice-principal. To create development within a working culture, a leader must enable interaction and the learning of the whole community. The creation of a learning culture requires systemic and systematic strategic management. When a community begins to evolve towards an organization that learns in teams, leadership enables dialogue and involvement.

The principal enables experiments and actions in the community. As a member of a team, the principal is involved in building a common understanding and discussing those enabling experiments in terms of the school's strategy. The principal has also the role of a learner. Informality and less hierarchy increase in the school management. Through team learning, people get to know each other as people, and see the school community from different viewpoints. In this, the principal needs support and strategic alignment, common view from coaches as well as from colleagues and superiors.

Often the principal's leadership role within the school community is quite lonely, and might suffer from stress when coping with everyday tasks. In the team organization model, power and actions in management are more evenly distributed, and the involvement of the working community is realized in teams. The common knowledge produced in teams works as the basis for decision making. Members of a community are strongly attached to their community when they can be genuinely involved. The community also formulates a school strategy together. Direction built together in dialogue helps everyone to concentrate on the essential, which brings well-being to the community.

In the project, our goal is to ponder how to increase children and young people's equality in learning and well-being at school. Team learning has been practiced in schools as an adult means of action. Deeper learning is achieved in teams, and the ability to see things from many perspectives grows as the team organization becomes multifunctional. In addition to the educational staff, youth workers and professionals in pupil welfare also work in schools. Working with these different professions in teams has been practiced during the project. Participants have reflected and experimented to investigate what happens when different professions from outside the immediate school environment come together with professions within the immediate school environment and become involved in dialogues in teams and build common understanding. To increase learning and well-being, there must be a stronger multi-actor approach in Finnish schools.

The Relevance of *On-the-Job* Learning

To enable equal basic education, action must be taken at each level of education and a new kind of thinking must be developed. There is no one easy solution for actions towards equal education, as many issues are interconnected. When facing complex issues, it is wise to seek solutions, trusting in interaction and common learning. A genuine experience of involvement and dialogue helps the community to notice and understand the connections important in development, and plan actions towards the jointly defined direction (Vartiainen & Raisio, 2020).

In the *Parasta ennen Project*, we wanted to seek a solution for the future of equal basic education in terms of school adults' learning and, in particular, the whole community's learning. The community's learning begins with an atmosphere of trust and a positive attitude towards learning. The second step is, through common dialogue, to define a problem to be solved, that is, what a community should learn together. Following this, the actions to be taken to reach the learning goals are laid out. Reflection is enabled through experiments, so as to understand the broader why and for whom we act. This kind of team learning process takes time, but common learning develops a common asset and resilience, which helps the community to cope more flexibly with the changes it faces. These factors affect the well-being of the whole community.

Our school system is based on a network of autonomous actors. In our project, we have been supporting this network. We did not have ready solutions to give to schools, but we have trusted that solutions would arise as the result of successful communication between the school's adults. Training sessions, support of management, support of co-creation, and drama education— these all have been supporting the learning that occurs in schools.

In the annual plan for the implementation of the local curriculum, schools describe their areas of development. In autumn, the everyday life of a school becomes so hectic that the areas of development get submerged by the problems encountered on a daily basis. To enable common learning, a structure is needed where every individual has the opportunity to learn and develop a view of where we are and where we are going. Changing situations and interconnected factors cause uncertainty. It is easier to cope with and understand uncertainty when thoughts are verbalized together. Common understanding in a community leads to actions towards goals. Interaction and actions in everyday life result in new characteristics and levels of action, which is shown as experience of involvement and learning through sharing, common responsibility, flexibility of one's role, natural shifting of leadership and situational solutions. A new characteristic might be, for instance, a positive atmosphere for learning (Vartiainen & Raisio, 2020).

By perceiving a common understanding, every adult working in a school can better see their work in relation to the whole system. Nevertheless, each individual learns at his/her own pace, and it is not possible to avoid tensions in common learning: how much discussion is needed to understand each other, and what things are immediately clearly defined, how much autonomy is there, and how strong is the need for guidance? A communities' preparedness to learn, ability to tackle new matters and cope with the incompleteness of processes increases through learning.

Communal learning also clearly requires an examination of management. Principals work very much alone in their schools and are often tied up with problems they face daily. In the *Parasta ennen Project*, principals are a part of a team in coaching sessions, but, of course, they have a role different from other team members as enablers of learning. To practice leading communal dialogue, principals receive support and training. Moreover, team coaches support them during the time between coaching sessions. During the whole project, the principals have received support around involvement, respectful co-creation process, and communication. In the communal learning process, the role of the principal is essential. The principal must have the motivation to learn together with the whole community. The common process must be respected so that there is enough time and space for training dialogue in everyday life, and so that the basic principles of dialogue work.

Team learning is at the core of the project. Team learning is a way of thinking and acting in which everyone is an active learner and actor. The goal of coaching is to support the school towards developing a working culture, not as a special project but as a part of the school's everyday activity. Team learning involving coaching aims at producing agency, building communal knowledge, forming common understanding, learning from active hands-on experiences, and developing reflective thinking. The task of the coaches is to help the school adults in this process. Team learning aids the understanding of the relevance of team organization in building a communal working culture.

Team learning is experiential learning. In order to learn, we need knowledge that enriches our dialogue. By reading and sharing our observations with others, we have the chance to think how we want everything to be. When we already have a common ground, we may begin a practical experiment. It is important that everyone in the work community tries it out in order to find a collective working culture. Every adult can decide the extent of the experiment by him/herself. Finding a common culture requires outlines and commitment but one prerequisite for commitment is a feeling of involvement. After experiments we can reflect on what we have learned together and separately. In the future, organizations must be able to create processes in which the whole community learns and develops together towards a way that is outlined together.

The goal of team coaching is for on-the-job learning to become a natural part of acting in the school community. It is the way to develop a shared understanding of what is important in our work. This kind of understanding increases motivation, which is one of the most important things that bind a work community together. Finding a common understanding demands regular dialogue in the work community. The goal of coaching is to help a community to get organized so that dialogue and shared learning are possible.

The way of thinking described earlier requires time and persistence, particularly in school communities where actors have become accustomed to having the broad pedagogic freedom to do their work independently. Learning together does not negate this, but it gives meaning to the things we do together.

The *Parasta ennen Project* team coaches have long experience in developing schools' working cultures. During the project, the team coaches have studied team coaching by participating in a training programme at Team Academy Global and by learning in practice. We have practiced an approach to coaching in which listening, reflecting, summarizing, and reviewing (rather than advising and giving instructions) are the central part of the working practice. It is our practice that we do not visit schools as authorities but rather as challengers or enablers of learning. The structure of singular coaching session that is repeated from one session to another has been essential for succeeding in coaching. Team coaches work in pairs, which has been a good decision. It has also been an effective way to learn coaching, because we have been able to reflect continually on our learning and debate with each other.

Alongside a busy and often task-oriented job at school, we need to revisit and hold on to those things that even global crises cannot subdue; humanity, a connection with others, resistance, and responsibility are values that can be built upon. The world needs to be made better and not more efficient! (Pölönen, 2019). That is why we invite all people working in school networks to participate in dialogue.

References

Haapaniemi, R., & Raina, L. (2014). *Rakenna oppiva ryhmä. Pedagogisen viihtymisen käsikirja.* Jyväskylä: PS-Kustannus.

Toivola, M., Peura, P. & Humaloja, M. (2017). *Flipped Learning. Käänteinen oppiminen.* Helsinki: Edita Publishing Oy.

Isaacs, W. (1999). *Dialogue and the art of thinking together.* New York: Bantam Doubleday Dell Publishing.

Norrena, J. (2019). *Oman oppimisen kapteeni.* Jyväskylä: PS-Kustannus.

Pölönen, P. (2019). *Tulevaisuuden lukujärjestys.* Otava: Editions in English Future Skills. (2021, Start Publishing).

Vartiainen, P., & Raisio, H. (2020). *Johtaminen kompleksisessa maailmassa. Viisautta pirullisten ongelmien kohtaamiseen.* Helsinki: Gaudeamus.

4 A Reflective Case Study on Using Team Academy Principles to Integrate a University-Based Business Incubator Service into the Mainstream Curriculum

Wendy Wu, Hock Tan, and Pauline Miller Judd

Introduction

According to the QAA (2018, p. 7), enterprise is *the generation and application of ideas, which are set within practical situations during a project or undertaking.* In 2017, Edinburgh Napier University, a modern university with approximately 18,000 students, developed an Innovation and Enterprise Strategy (Miller Judd & Laing, 2017) focused on enhancing enterprise activities both within the formal curriculum and as extracurricular activities. Building on this strategy, this pilot project sought to explore ways that the university's incubation hub could work with academic staff on projects embedded in the formal Business School curriculum.

Bright Red Triangle (BRT) is the hub for innovation and enterprise practice at Edinburgh Napier University which supports staff, students, and alumni to develop enterprise skills and capture business opportunities. BRT has followed traditional models of university incubators, supporting student and graduate entrepreneurs as well as research and development. This support is provided through business advice, on a one-to-one basis and through workshops and online activities. BRT engages with entrepreneurial activities and helps bridge the gaps between the university education and real-world business.

BRT grew out of Edinburgh Napier Business School (ENBS), scaling up its service to provide support to all six schools in the university. Given its root and originality from ENBS, the natural connection provides a culture ground for developing new initiatives. The appointment of a New Dean in 2018 reshaped the ENBS strategy to focus on "empowerment, enterprise, and employability" for all. The strategy has not only become the base for a

DOI: 10.4324/9781003163176-5

change in management but also to position ENBS in the heart of the industry and society.

The aim of this chapter is to reflect on lessons learned during this three-year pilot project focusing on student and staff learning and the micro embedding of Team Academy principles in joint enterprise projects.

Why and How the Journey Started

Through observation, reflection and informal feedback concerning teaching activities and business advising, several enterprise service gaps were identified:

(a) Reviewing students' business plans showed their understanding of business lacked depth. Overseas students interested in a Tier 1 graduate visas require innovative and viable business plans and those submitted often demonstrated superficial understanding of business and a lack of ability to apply conceptual ideas to real-world situations.

(b) Some academic colleagues were using dated theoretical case studies and lacked the channels to approach guest speakers from business to enhance the real-world learning experience of students.

(c) Students either realized the value of incubator activities late in their studies or struggled to find the time to engage with BRT activities. BRT often struggled to get sufficient attendees to participate in their practice-oriented workshops, with student attendance being disappointing and/or sporadic.

d) Also, there were perceived gaps in curriculum and support for social enterprise.[1] Students appeared less informed of the real-world practices of social innovation movements such as climate change, global citizenship, and equality. This highlighted that the pace of theoretical knowledge development did not match the real-world needs and reflects Billett's (2010) assertions that higher education's emphasis on educational provision privileges more traditional learning.

Students are increasingly restricted with time to balance work, social life, study, and the extra-curricular nature of the business incubator services was identified as a restriction to student utilization. Stuart et al. noted that *differences in ECA (extra-curricular activity) engagement are evident between 'traditional' and what may be defined more widely as 'widening participation/non-traditional' students* (2011, p. 212). As Edinburgh Napier University has a large proportion of non-traditional students, these challenges with extracurricular engagement highlighted that the development of embedded "real-world" learning could enhance learning outcomes, expand opportunities for students to engage with start-up businesses and ultimately increase the success of both BRT and student outcomes.

Consideration was given to constructing a model which allowed students to participate in experiential learning, through which they could discover their passions, understand how new knowledge is constructed, and use creativity to develop innovative solutions. This model created an open learning environment where students could apply theory through critical review and interaction with business/industry expertise, challenge status quos, challenge themselves, and recognize how to lead their self-learning process.

Contemplating those changes led to exploration of two approaches namely Team Academy (TA) principles and Open Innovation (Chesbrough et al., 2006). The TA approach is based on learning by doing, working with customers, peer learning, and applying theory to practice (Halttunen, 2006). In open innovation, Chesbrough et al. (2006) highlight that to gain a competitive advantage, organizations ought to create a knowledge flow to allow outsiders in and insiders out. These approaches highlighted that a business incubator could be the catalyst for such knowledge flow between the formal and informal learning opportunities. As such, embedding elements of BRT in the Business School curriculum was identified as a potential solution to the service gaps identified, addressing the challenges many students had to engage with BRT and place their academic learning in the context of real-world challenges.

To enable this, BRT business adviser (author Wu) and academic lecturer (author Tan) agreed to explore a collaboration to develop an integrated co-creation framework leading to a 3-year pilot project.

Developing the Project

The trajectory of the project was in three stages:

1. Dive in
2. In-project learning and development by doing
3. Championing for mainstreaming

Two Business School undergraduate modules were selected for engagement with the pilot: Business Strategy and Sustainable Development, a final year module, and Introduction to Business Ethics and Sustainability, a second-year module.

Project learning objectives were aligned with the United Nations (n.d.) SDG17 from which six key aligned areas were identified:

- Digital innovation and developing capacity for and within local communities

- Challenges of climate change including energy, consumption, and climate change impacts
- Gender equality and female empowerment
- Social capital and inequality
- Social investment models
- Community lending banks

Targeting these areas, selected thought leaders were invited to brief students on real-world practice and challenges. Students were then assigned into groups according to how their interests aligned and student groups had the opportunity to develop professional working relationships with the thought leaders.

Three levels of possible student outputs were anticipated:

- A reflective piece of work. This could be either used for personal development or used towards summative assessments in their module.
- A consultancy output. At the time this was not possible to be assessed within either associated module. However, it helped bridge the gap between curriculum and incubator support.
- For those who developed a desire to engage with more entrepreneurial activities, they could go to BRT to discuss setting up their own business based on their learning from the challenge.

Year 1: Dive In

Given constraints of time, resources, and limited ability to change existing programme structures, the project team adopted a micro implementation of the Team Academy methodology by primarily using "learning by doing" and enhancing "human relationships", embedding constructive dialogue but not coaching. Students were briefed and introduced to the Isaacs' dialogue model at the outset (Isaacs, 1999) to develop empathic listening and engagement to support the exploration of diverse perspectives from different stakeholders.

The project was designed for students to participate voluntarily though their modules. Initially it was anticipated there might be 100 students but only 24 signed up. Students were expected to sign up in groups according to their shared interests, but the numbers posed challenges given the levels of knowledge diversity. The original plan to be a competitive enterprise with the best team awarded a prize at the end of the session was dropped due to numbers and inequalities across the teams.

After the students engaged in immediate learning, observation, and reflection, the activity shifted to a career-oriented talk from a social enterprise leader. This change was driven by students' interests and desire to understand what inspired them and why they had given up a corporate role to run a social enterprise. Students found this level of engagement stimulating and it highlighted the need to understand the job market and engage with industry professionals to gain relevant employability skills.

Abandoning the original plan and diving in with the "live discussion" was possible because of the trust established between the two project collaborators. This demonstrated the importance of flexibility and improvisation to enhance and maximize the learning experience. The project collaborators witnessed the power of learner determined learning and the benefits of learners driving the learning agendas. On reflection, this shows the benefit of facilitators themselves approaching tasks with an open mind and being willing to continually engage in exploration and learning. With that mindset there were learning opportunities for *teachers, students,* and *speakers* before, during, and after the session. The receptive mindset also created an open and trusting environment in which students and participants took ownership of their own learning journey, and where passion and curiosity played an important role in new knowledge creation.

Unexpected Results

The initial dive-in cultivated an environment for self-determined learning and authenticity of academic leadership emerged as an important enabler. Authenticity here refers to the importance for any professionals, including academic colleagues and external speakers, to bring their whole body of knowledge to the teaching and learning context.

There were three key take-aways from the first year. First, the project generated a significant workload for the staff involved, including project design, stakeholder engagement, recruitment, logistic liaison, project planning, execution, evaluation, and contingency development. However, it also provided interesting learning in understanding each other's approaches and perspectives which provided a foundation to build the trust and validate the integration concept.

The second learning point was reflection on the root purpose of the project, highlighting the need to empower students and delegate tasks to them as the core of their learning and doing practice. This was further developed and implemented in year 2 of the experiment.

The third learning point was that the improvisational experience reinforced how important the focus on leaners' needs is. The establishment of an environment where learning has been interacted and "negotiated" with other learners and participants is vital in supporting those needs. It reinforced the idea that learning takes place in multiple levels of time and space and demonstrated the emergence of a virtual equal learning community where everyone has an equal footing and the teacher is merely a learning facilitator.

Beyond the anticipated outcomes of the year 1 pilot, a tangible output was generated through this collaboration. One graduate initiated a creative concept during the project which was awarded an Innovation Voucher from Interface. This enabled the graduate to test, validate, and prototype the idea in a chemistry material lab, working in collaboration with senior academic researchers from the School of Engineering and the Built Environment.

Year 2: In-Project Learning and Development by Doing

Reflecting on the learning from year 1, a framework was developed to keep the focus on team challenges but embedding "being, knowing, doing and creating".

Building on the TA learning model, based on Nonaka and Takeuchi's knowledge management model, the framework was designed to integrate

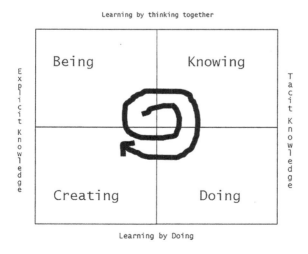

Figure 4.1 Four Domains of Knowledge Integration

Source: authors' own

personal development (being) and business incubator service (doing and creating) into mainstream curriculum learning (knowing). These domains are achieved through the tackling of real-world challenges.

- *Being* – Students first need to explore their entrepreneurial passions and capacities by exploring their inner world to find what motivates them. This will determine which project they choose to work on.
- *Knowing* – Once students understand their own skill sets and passions, they are introduced to entrepreneurial thinking and processes, applying conceptual theories they have "learnt" through traditional classroom-style learning.
- *Doing* – Here students get into small project groups and start immersing into themselves in real-world challenges. This involves participating in the engagement conference and entering into debates with real-world professionals. During this period, staff from the incubator delivers workshops on how to apply the knowledge when addressing real-world challenges. Tool kits are provided to put into practice what they have learnt.
- *Creating* – This is the final stage of synchronizing knowledge and learning. Student groups are required to present their proposed solution in both a short written report and an oral presentation. They then take questions from other groups and teachers.

The tipping point for the project came when the collaborative facilitators invited the students to take on ownership of the project, including the learning design, organization, and defining challenge activities and communication strategy. This led to a mini-conference being organized by the student teams, in which over 80 students engaged.

The learning engagement format was changed to motivate students to take their own initiative:

(a) To provide a learning experience to make students realize that learning takes place not only in the classroom but also through engagement with the outside world
(b) To provide a showcase that enables students to understand how the civic society operates, enabling them to think about what role they can play in the community
(c) To inspire students to understand how social enterprises are built on the passion of entrepreneurs, how to leverage support from corporate sources to make a positive impact, and most importantly developing entrepreneurial skills to turn a challenge into an opportunity

As a complementary activity, a learning expedition was organized by a staff member to a third sector organization. Those students who engaged in the learning expedition found it a useful experience enabling them to engage with social entrepreneurs in their own environment.

Critical Reflection

Reflection on year 2 suggested that empowering students to own the project provided a crucial change in manifesting the importance of engaging in self-directed learning, and establishing a learning environment which integrated passion, mission, profession, and vocation. However, it also posed a challenge in engaging stakeholders at multiple levels with the teaching and learning framework, as well as developing a quality assurance framework of integrating the four elements of "being", "knowing", "doing" and "creating".

The second iteration of the project highlighted resource challenges. Firstly, the timetabling of crucial activities was still challenging, and consideration needed to be given as to whether attendance was made compulsory. Also, students asked whether funds were available to test innovative ideas for their group projects but unfortunately, there were no financial resources available.

Accreditation and acknowledgement of student engagement was also highlighted as an issue. As with many higher education institutions, Edinburgh Napier is engaging with higher education achievement reports (HEAR). However, the issue is not only how to record the achievement and experience in the transcript, but also how to evaluate diverse participants' engagement, experience, and quality assurance at each stage of development. It highlights the question to what extent non-academic engagement can be valued in a meaningful and validated manner.

Year 3: Championing for Mainstreaming

Consolidating the learning experience of the first 2 years, the year 3 experience made a significant leap. Early evidence of the project was presented to the Dean who was supportive of its development, and the project gained various championing bodies both in and outwith the university. In the third year it was decided this would remain a student led project enabling staff to move to a more supportive role. BRT services were also for the first time formally timetabled into the curriculum and there was a substantial increase in the number of students involved as the project became compulsory for final year students.

Students were invited to put themselves forward for leadership roles to support the conference which focused on ending poverty, the first goal of UN SDGs. Preceding the conference, three preparation workshops were organized for the students. The first one was on deep listening and dialogue, second on showcasing by social enterprises, and third on ideation. The conference was attended by over 250 delegates, of which 205 were students. As a result, in 2020, the project generated 65 student team projects with teams ranging from 3 to 5 participants. The teams were self-selecting and were given some staff support through the module leader and BRT. The nature of the projects they engaged with ranged from establishing instant ID cards for homeless people, to developing a computer application to connect institutional partners, and tracing relevant services for homeless people. BRT awarded the top three student projects support to continue their business development.

Additionally, elements of assessment were embedded in each stage of the project. Prior to the conference, students were asked to pitch and present a poster based on the use of business model canvas (source) to peer groups, which were assessed. At the conference poster exhibition, students were asked to practice their pitching skills to articulate their solutions for the issues and proposal for implementation. BRT and academic staff members jointly conducted the summative assessment. Moreover, a competition was organized, and the best three student teams were invited to pitch their ideas at the conference. Additionally, the students with the best ideas were invited to participate in an international entrepreneurial event co-hosted by BRT with the Strascheg Center for Entrepreneurship (SCE) at the Munich University of Applied Sciences (MUAS).

Challenges

One of the biggest challenges was how to implement the TA principles within an existing structured course module. This requires the participants, including lecturers and speakers, to understand the basic concepts and TA principles holistically, ensuring its benefits can be maximized. TA principles were introduced to the module leaders through discussion on learning design, delivery, and evaluation. However, given the limited time, it was not possible to introduce TA fully to other participants prior to the sessions. Instead, the ethos and principles of TA was introduced by the module leaders throughout the sessions. This shared understanding took time to embed. It is only with the third iteration that the principles of learning by doing, working with customers, peer learning, and applying theory to practice (Halttunen, 2006) were fully embedded. The nature of the project and the number of students involved meant that aspects of the TA approach, such as team coaching, were not possible.

TA principles were adapted to address the segmented issues with an intention to bring a holistic solution. However, to a certain degree, it was required to be de-holistic and broken down, as the TA methodology needed to fit the project's purpose. Therefore, partial efforts only lead to partial results. To fully address the challenges facing universities, industry, and societies, there is a need to draw the bigger picture together to shape a shared purpose, shared development agenda, and the ownership of a shared journey and space together.

More explicitly, it means a University-based incubator can play a stronger role in the new knowledge creation process within an existing curriculum, supporting not just ideation but also the development of production and services into the market space. The knowledge facilitation has also meant that more on-shelf academic knowledge can be better used for real-world challenges. The knowledge flow needs to be created from an upward, and downward, inward, and outward spiral process involving individuals, teams, and the university as an organization.

The model of being-knowing-doing-creating (see Figure 4.2) is inspired by author Wu's woven journey in meditation, business advising, and life. It has also been significantly influenced by the knowledge creation theory of Nonaka and Takeuchi (1995) and the Open Innovation Theory of Chesbrough et al.,(2006).

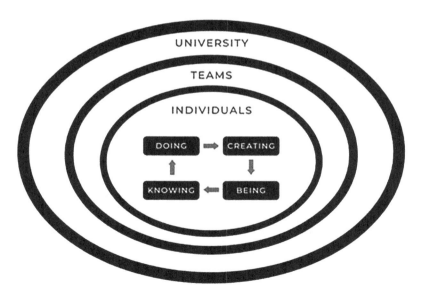

Figure 4.2 Knowledge Flow Spiral Process
Source: Authors' own

The importance of a coaching role and dialogue in these types of projects can never be underestimated. It can be utilized for the benefits of students, but also to develop the efficiency of the staff team. True dialogue can enhance their interaction, making it more productive which can lead to a transformative change. So far, TA approaches have only been applied in micro ways. Both Wu and Miller Judd are trained as TA coaches and implemented TA principles in areas such as problem solving, real life learning, dialogue, and team learning. It is believed that if TA can be fully utilized, specifically to cultivate future change makers and future shapers, it will be for the benefit of the university and wider community. TA principles have inspired the project initiator (Wu) to influence other module leaders to implement a co-creating impactful curriculum through challenge-based learning and embed the university-based incubator service in the mainstream curriculum. Part of the solution going forward might be using existing expertise to train academics to apply TA principles. By doing this, it is anticipated the range of outputs will proliferate and enhance a win-win situation for all stakeholders.

The embedding of this project in the curriculum happened quicker than expected, supported by the arrival of a new Dean of the Business School whose vision included bringing "empowerment, employment, and entrepreneurship" together. From multiple dimensions, the Dean was convinced of the value created by the project, seeing that it has contributed to a culture change at the Business School and created the possibility of a unique marketing proposition. Discussion is in progress with regard to how to scale up this co-creation model across the Business School curriculum. There are three fundamental challenges faced:

1. The need for designated resources if this model is to be applied across the whole curriculum. Given contextual differences, this requires a suitable mainstream model to be devised and adapted to suit individual modules.
2. Scaling up may require structural changes to the curriculum to allow for the flexibility and capacity to absorb emerging needs of students and learners, given the fluid nature of live projects.
3. Once the scaled-up model is determined, the approach to interaction and engagement with external stakeholders will need to be determined to maximize resources and impact.

Impact and Conclusion

The project has had several impacts including:

- enhanced cultivation of students' entrepreneurial development;
- embedded entrepreneurship into the mainstream curriculum and changed the learning environment;
- enhanced learning experience through integrating service provision and linking career, academic, and personal development;
- a tangible outcome of a successful innovation voucher[2] application supporting a graduate venture to partner with academic experts to develop a prototype of a new sustainable product.[3]

The student feedback suggested that the TA approach of live real-world projects enhanced the quality-of-service provision as well as enriched the learning experience. The insights gained will feed into enhancing the entrepreneurial framework. Further testing and scale up will provide capacity to generate new knowledge particularly in how best to adapt the model to different situations.

Empowering students, peer-to-peer learning, and cross-sector learning communities using TA principles has also helped develop student leadership and entrepreneurial abilities. The experiential learning has provided students with first-hand understanding of new knowledge creation, encouraging them to be active learners, and giving them skills and confidence to tackle new problems. However, resource limitations have constrained the maximization of learning outcomes and team coaching input could enhance outcomes for student teams.

One of the key learnings for staff members lies in how to cultivate entrepreneurship engagement and the integrated model has provided a starting point for enhanced integration both within and outwith the University. However, whilst BRT demonstrated how it can add value in an *academic* setting and act as an agent of change, the model needs to be further developed in different contexts and with different actors.

Three key takeaways from the project are:

- The project confirmed that creating a learning community and giving students ownership based on TA principles stimulates new knowledge, enhance the ownership of learning, and empower and engage students. This can create transformative change.
- The establishment of cross disciplinary/cross sector groups can add significant value to curriculum design, development, and delivery. Creating an integrated learning model, bringing academics, service professionals, and experts from industry and business together can create a win-win situation enhancing knowledge transfer.
- If prepared to take risks and think innovatively, Higher Education institutions can develop new pedagogical strategies which help produce future ready graduates who are agile, adaptive, and resilient.

Notes

1 Social enterprise is defined in a broader sense, referring to purpose-oriented businesses. It includes businesses in the third sector and beyond in the UK context.
2 The Innovation Voucher Scheme is a UK Government Initiative which provides up to £5,000 of funding for academic assistance in the development of business projects.
3 Algae Limited | Interface Knowledge Connection (interface-online.org.uk).

References

Billett, S. (2010). The perils of confusing lifelong learning and lifelong education. *International Journal of Lifelong Education, 29*(4), 401–413. https://doi.org/10.1080/02601370.2010.488803

Chesbrough, H., Vanhaverbeke, W., & West, J. (Eds.). (2006). *Open innovation: Researching a new paradigm.* Oxford: Oxford University Press on Demand.

Halttunen, J. (2006). Team Academy—award winning entrepreneurship education from Jyvaskyla, Finland. In Presentation at OECD/IMHE Conference, Copenhagen, 16 October. www.oecd.org/education/imhe/37544053.pdf

Isaacs, W. (1999). *Dialogue and the art of thinking together.* New York: Currency, Doubleday Press.

Miller Judd, P., & Laing, S. (2017). *Innovation and enterprise strategy.* Edinburgh: Edinburgh Napier University. https://staff.napier.ac.uk/services/principal/strategy/Documents/Innovation%20and%20Enterprise%20Strategy.pdf

Nonaka, I., & Takeuchi, H. (1995). *The knowledge-creating company: How Japanese companies create the dynamics of innovation.* Oxford: Oxford University Press.

Quality Assurance Agency (QAA). (2018). *Enterprise and Entrepreneurship Education: Guidance for UK higher education providers.* Gloucester: The Quality Assurance Agency for Higher Education. www.qaa.ac.uk/docs/qaas/enhancement-and-development/enterprise-and-entrpreneurship-education-2018.pdf?sfvrsn=15f1f981_8

Stuart, M., Lido, C., Morgan, J., & May, S. (2011). The impact of engagement with extracurricular activities on the student experience and graduate outcomes for widening participation populations. *Active Learning in Higher Education, 12*(3), 203–215. https://doi.org/10.1177/1469787411415081

United Nations. (n.d.). www.un.org/sustainabledevelopment/sustainable-development-goals/

5 Educating Creativity for Innovation – Unprecedented Challenge in Japan

Hajime Imamura

Introduction

The encounter between our new department, GINOS (Department of Global Innovation Studies), and the Mondragon MTA, which occurred at an extremely serendipitous time, may prove to be historic in retrospect in terms of achieving its goal of compensating for the lack of entrepreneurship in Japan.

Japan's human resource development system, which achieved high economic growth, performed extremely well in building human capital through long-term employment and internal human resource development modelled on that of large-scale corporations. Within the pyramidal internal labour market formed by internal promotion, the systematic job rotation formed skills with many company-specific elements. This is the so-called membership type employment system.

However, with the intensification of global competition and innovation, long-term human resource development plans are no longer able to provide the necessary human resources, and an increasing number of Japanese companies have recently declared that they cannot maintain lifetime employment and are shifting from membership-based employment to job-based employment.

This is our starting point to create GINOS to revitalize Japanese innovation ecosystem from the human resource point of view (GINOS, 2020). With the evidence below in our GIC (Center for Global Innovation Studies) ranking initiated from 2019.

Implications for Revitalizing Japanese Innovation Human Resource Development from the Findings of GIC Innovation Ranking

The Center for Global Innovation Studies (GIC) has selected 58 indicators, including productivity per worker and the number of technical experts in

DOI: 10.4324/9781003163176-6

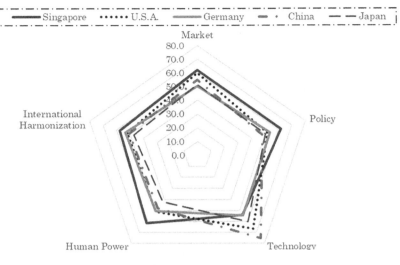

Figure 5.1   Five Components Diagram
Source: GIC (2020)

R&D to compare and verify the progress level of innovation of each country. These indicators are considered to be contributors to the growth of GDP per capita in the long term. A high correlation between the past growth rates and the rankings based on these indicators was found (GIC, 2020).

These indicators have been grouped into five categories, International Harmonization, Market, Technology, Human Power, and Market Policy, and into 18 subcategories in order to be able to make categorical comparison per country (GIC, 2020).

The chart below shows a comparison of the five major items of innovation of the five target countries (Singapore [rank 1], USA [rank 9], Germany [rank 20], China [rank 15], and Japan [rank 32]).

From this chart, Singapore is at a well-balanced point; the United States and China are far ahead in term of technology, while Japan has a particularly low Human Power. The decomposition of the sources of low human power shows the strong motivation of starting our GINOS human resource education program.

Japanese Poor Human Power for Innovation

By decomposing the contents of Human Power and Market that includes Innovative human resource variables, we found the following:

(1) In terms of the breakdown of human capital, Japan's scores for *youthfulness of the population (observed indicator: ratio of working-age population)* and *spirit of challenge (observed indicator: trends in student entrepreneurship) are* both quite low. The latter can be addressed through educational reform and will be an important issue for Japan in the years ahead

(2) In the *Diversity* category, Japan's score for *Acceptance of foreigners (immigrants and foreign students)* was considerably lower than Singapore, Germany, and the United States. The acceptance of foreign nationals is often called for in response to labour shortages, but also should be viewed from the perspective of accepting high-level human resources and diversifying society

(3) The score for *education* was lower than the average of all countries. In the breakdown of sub-items, Japan scored above average in *basic academic ability (PISA, math literacy, science literacy)*, but not enough in *recurrent education (participation rate in higher education among people aged 25 and over)* and *university ranking*. In addition, Japan's score for *foreign language proficiency (TOEFLE-iBT)* is the lowest among the five countries in focus although Japan has been making various attempts to improve its English proficiency,

(4) Entrepreneurship (Venture capital investment, Corporate innovation capacity, Willingness of firms to adopt new technologies) and Investment Capability (Savings rate, Listed market capitalization, Change in number of listed companies) are at good levels, but the Start-up indicator (New business registration and Ease of starting a business) is low, ranking only fourth among the five countries analysed. This is consistent with the low rate of business start-ups in Japan. This suggests that structural factors, such as the rigidity of the labour market and industrial structure, are at play in the lack of entrepreneurship, even though the level of investment capacity (ample funds) and entrepreneurship (as for business corporations), which are important factors for entrepreneurship, is not very low

Society 5.0 for Science and Technology for Human Centred Society

First of all, the definition of Society 5.0 is as follows: *a human-centred society (Society) that achieves both economic development and solutions to social issues through a system that highly integrates cyberspace (virtual space) and physical space (real space)*(Cabinet Office, 2016). In other words, the idea is to shift from policies that focus on economic growth to policies that are compatible with solving social issues, and to deploy and utilize highly integrated virtual and real space technologies to support this shift.

According to the 5th Science and Technology Basic Plan (Cabinet Office, 2016) proposes Society 5.0 as the main keyword of this plan and explain this plan as follows. The Internet of Things (IoT) will *overcome these challenges and difficulties by connecting all people and things, sharing a variety of knowledge and information, and creating new value that has never been seen before.* In addition, artificial intelligence (AI) will *provide necessary information when it is needed, and technologies such as robots and self-driving cars will overcome issues such as the declining birth-rate and aging population, depopulation of rural areas, and disparity between the rich and the poor.* In other words, the emphasis is on social transformation and problem solving.

And, the 5th Science and Technology Basic Plan explains why they should have combined both economic and social aspects under the name of the Society 5.0, which is as follows. As a result of continued economic development, *demand for energy and food is increasing, life expectancy is increasing, and the population is aging,* while *intensifying international competition, concentration of wealth, and inequality among regions* are occurring. In addition to the above, the report mentions *reducing greenhouse gas (GHG) emissions, increasing food production and reducing food loss, curbing social costs associated with the aging of society, promoting sustainable industrialization, redistributing wealth, and correcting regional disparities* as *complex social issues that need to be resolved in conflict (trade-off) with these issues.* Above all, the report recognizes that it is difficult to achieve both economic development and the resolution of social issues under the current social system.

Will it be possible to achieve both economic development and the resolution of social issues by incorporating new technological advances such as IoT, robotics, artificial intelligence (AI), and big data into all industries and social life? In addition, it will also lead to the achievement of the UN's Sustainable Development Goals (SDGs). It can be said that this development of realizing both economic and social development from a global perspective is a change of direction from the past in Japan (focus on economic and technological innovation) and aims at realizing both social and human innovation in the context of international cooperation, which is truly the direction of *global innovation.*

Evolution of the Innovation Ecosystem Towards the Realization of Society 5.0

In response to these policy proposals for Society 5.0, various organizations and companies have begun to work together. Among them, the Keidanren

(Japan Business Federation) has redefined the Cabinet Office's proposal for Society 5.0 as *a society that solves social issues and creates value through the fusion of digital innovation and the imagination and creativity of diverse people* and has issued a series of proposals (Keidanren, 2018). The stagnation of the *movement of human resources* between companies, public institutions, and universities is an issue that needs to be resolved in order to promote industry-university collaboration.

There is a noteworthy report issued by Keizai Doyukai (2015) that presents the challenges for realizing an open innovation ecosystem that activates horizontal connections in Japan. The report shows the top 10 countries in terms of both inward and outward direct investment. While Japan is the top country in terms of outward direct investment, its inward direct investment is at an extremely low level, close to the bottom. In a nutshell, this indicates that Japan is not seen as an attractive destination for direct investment by other countries, and this has not changed at all in a long time.

Keizai Doyukai (2015) identifies strengthening human resources as the biggest challenge and proposes four measures: (1) the ability to accept and utilize diversity, (2) fostering a culture that allows failure, (3) changing mindsets, and (4) English language skills to take advantage of global best practices. To achieve these goals, the government needs to review its regulations and systems, and the top priorities are (1) a systemic reform to increase the mobility of human resources and (2) taxation to attract highly skilled human resources.

This shows that the realization of an open innovation ecosystem and the human resources that support it are inextricably linked. As will be discussed in the next section, the Toyo University Center for Global Innovation Studies (GIC) index analysis suggests a solution to this problem, but before that, if we examine the reasons why there is little inward FDI into Japan, a major factor is *human resources*. JETRO (2019) report on Investment in Japan 2019 illustrates the issue clearly. The top two obstacles for foreign companies to do business in Japan are *difficulty in securing human resources* and *difficulty in communicating in foreign languages*. Furthermore, according to the Persol Research Institute (2019), Japanese people's awareness of independence and entrepreneurship is the lowest compared to comparable countries in Asia. This makes Japan an extremely unattractive country in terms of human resources for the establishment of a global and open innovation ecosystem.

The Ministry of Economy, Trade, and Industry's "FY2020 Global Startup Ecosystem Enhancement Project (Global Venture Summit)" is aiming in almost the same direction, as summarized by the following two statements in the project objectives and outline (METI, 2018): to realize Society 5.0, start-ups, which are the bearers of innovation, are important, but the number of unicorns companies originating from Japan remains small. However, there are still few *unicorns* companies from Japan. On the other hand, competition in the start-up ecosystem is intensifying among countries and regions around the world. To improve Japan's international competitiveness under the fourth Industrial Revolution, it is urgent to strengthen the start-up ecosystem and create a series of start-ups that can win in the world.

In this project (CREATOYO Global Creativity Week) we will invite leading executives, entrepreneurs, venture capitalists, and institutional investors from around the world to participate in the Global Venture Summit (tentative name) (hereinafter referred to as *the Summit*) to attract foreign investors to invest in Japan's top companies, promote open innovation between large companies and start-ups, and foster a Japanese style innovation culture.

An Educational Solution to Solve Human Development Challenges in Japan

What kind of ecosystem for fostering human resources for innovation will be created through collaboration among universities, government, and business, and what kind of entities (human resources and organizations) will be expected to appear and participate as new players? This is not something that can be achieved only by policy-making concepts and support plans, nor by promoting and accumulating individual research at universities.

To achieve the necessary ecosystem for innovative human resources, universities play a central role in the future to establish a collaborative educational platform that combines university education with corporations, government agencies, international organizations, and non-profit organizations and provide creative and innovative graduates. Amid many universities and departments participating to this ecosystem. a major *raison d'être* for the development of GINOS as the flagship of Toyo University's *Top global universities (SGU)* in the Toyo University Global Diamond Initiative (MEXT, 2017). This project is part of the formation of a research and education hub to create a global ecosystem for the education of innovative and entrepreneurial human resources.

The education in the Department of Global Innovation Studies (GINOS) in the Faculty of global and Regional Studies (GRS) and the research on global human resources in the Research Center for Global Innovation Studies (GIC) form part of this project. In addition to this, Toyo University aims to conduct research, analysis, and practice of human resource development in cooperation with advanced universities and research institutes overseas, focusing on the bottom-up and horizontal innovation generation process, which is different from the conventional Japanese perspective on innovation.

We would like to introduce the outline of this project below and expand the results of our educational practice and human resource development research from GINOS and GIC.

GINOS Global Entrepreneurship Education Programme

In 2016, Toyo University formulated a new action plan, *Beyond 2020*, as a vision to create an education hub for innovation and entrepreneurship. The keywords of the vision are *Globalization, Innovation Creativity* and *Human Value* under the guidance of the Chairman Fukukawa (Toyo University, 2016), then chairman of the board of directors, explained the background and aims of the project as follows: *The power of the Japanese people is what is needed to creatively solve the problems that Japan and the world are facing, and to open up the future for a global society. In addition, the philosophy of Creativity and Human Value, which is the source of Creative Human Power, will support this. Toyo University will evolve to continue to be a centre of education and research that opens up the future of Japan and the world by nurturing 'people' who can think deeply and boldly about 'what the future of Japan and international society should be' from a broad perspective.*

It must be emphasized here that the concept of Beyond 2020 is not something that emerged with the adoption of SGU, but it is unique to Toyo University.

The Department of Global Innovation Studies (GINOS) was newly established in 2017 with the aim of transforming students into globally competitive human resources who can create innovations everywhere in the world. Advocating the basic principle of *cultivating horizontally oriented global talents in the spirit of philosophy that forms the basis of dialogue with people and earth* the Department aims to foster leaders who meet global standards by providing students with dialogue-based problem-solving education in a diversity-friendly environment where all sessions are given in English. In addition, all Japanese students are required to study abroad for one or two semesters, and around 30% of GINOS students are international students.

Although this department is of an unprecedented one for Toyo University, its prototype can date back to the University's foundation days about 130 years ago when Toyo University was established by Enryo Inoue, a *Travelling Philosopher* who travelled around the world three times and walked around Japan to give lectures on his experiences abroad for 27 years from 1890 to 1919. He lectured about the application of philosophy to social education as well as the practical learning of Fukuzawa Yukichi, the founder of Keio University. Inheriting this spirit of the *Travelling Founder*,

GINOS has just started as a completely new canvas that provides students with education based on the experience of *Travel, Play, and Dialogue.*

(1) Travel: Entrepreneurship and Innovation Learning Journey in Collaboration with MTA

First, through *Travelling* students are challenged to develop their own capability to take action and resolve problems based on tolerance and understanding of global diversity in cultural, social, economic, historical, environmental, and other contexts, in collaboration with diverse agents with different backgrounds. Japanese students are required to study outside Japan for one or two semesters from the second half of the second year and are offered various other opportunities for travelling soon after they enter the department. For example, the *Entrepreneurship and Innovation Learning Journey* in collaboration with MTA assigns students the task of visiting certain countries (usually one week in Bilbao), having frequent dialogues, and finally proposing a business model or policy proposals. We will offer students many other learning opportunities having *travel* choices.

We started our first Learning Journey to Basque and Florence in 2018 from February 23 to March 11 composed of below activities aiming at to develop the students' competence on Creativity, Socio economical values, Teamwork, Entrepreneurship mindset, and International business culture.

The second Learning Journey (February–March 2019) took place in the Basque Country and Madrid, Spain. The nine students were divided into two teams using a personality test, and each team was given a challenge to solve. By limiting the number of students to nine, we were able to provide more guidance and communication, and each student was able to achieve significant results.

One of the main reasons for success was the human network, planning, and negotiation skills of Mr. John Ander Musatadi, CEO of JAM Global, who was in charge of the tour. In addition, the warm and enthusiastic response of the students at the Mondragon University MTA Bilbao and Madrid had an extremely positive effect on the GINOS students. The visit to the business school of the University of Deusto, with which we have an international exchange agreement, was also made possible by the generosity of the host institution, the favourable campus environment, and the workshops given by the lecturers of the incubation centre of the university.

Creativity for innovation is not just about knowledge and skills, but also about incorporating a wide range of elements such as art and culture to inspire

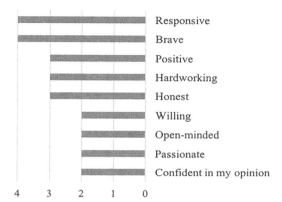

Figure 5.2 Top 9 Developed Personalities
Source: GIC (2018)

creativity. In Bilbao, visits to the Guggenheim Museum, the Vizcaya Bridge (a World Heritage Site), and Guernica as a model of democracy as well as the tragedy of Guernica, encouraged the spiritual growth of the students. In Madrid, the Queen Sofia Museum, which has the original of Picasso's Guernica, and the world-famous Prado Museum's collection inspired design thinking skills. In addition, the challenge of solving the problems faced by the city of Madrid through actual fieldwork in the city fostered the ability to see the city broadly as a target for problem solving. In this respect, Madrid provided the perfect environment.

There were significant outcomes to students from the Journey:

(1) Personality: considering the result in Figure 5.2, it seems that the students developed their personality by confronting challenges during the learning journey.

(2) Soft skills: through the leaning journey, students developed communication skill, stress management, design thinking, and other soft skills to enhance their creativity.

(3) Facing and solving challenges: students felt they were facing challenges around their English ability, knowledge, critical thinking, and communication skills. Students achieved to overcome those challenges to enhance their creativity and survive in the Learning Journey.

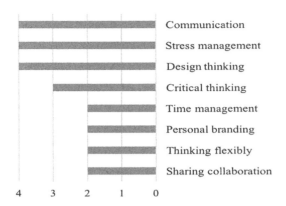

Figure 5.3 Top 8 Developed Soft Skills
Source: GIC (2018)

(2) Play: English Communication Exercise Using Acting Training Under the Instruction of Japanese Actress and Director in London

Play is also a basis for our education. Newly enrolled students may not have a high English level yet, but we encourage them to be eager to communicate actively in English. Good communication entails ability to make themselves fully understood by others, and the foundation for communication skills is around their capability to *Play* and achieve an interactive understanding of diverse context.

The Department of Global Innovation welcomed Yuri Yamanaka, an actress working in the UK, for a theatre workshop entitled *English Communication Exercise Using Acting Training*. This class is organized by Hajime Imamura and conducted by You-Ri Yamanaka who has been working as an Actress, Voiceover Artist, Movement Director, and Acting Teacher in the UK, Europe, and Japan. It is a practical training that combines various vocalization methods and the expressive power of movements.

Communication and presentation skills are essential in our globalized world, both at work and in daily life. In this course, we will practice to let our thoughts go whilst using our heart, body, voice, words, and mind organically. The most important thing is, "to be understood" rather than, "to

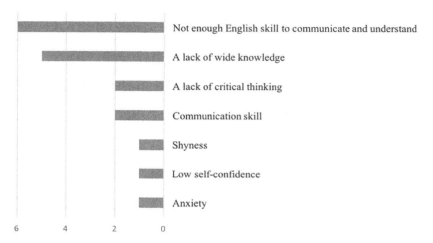

Figure 5.4 Discovered Challenges
Source: GIC (2018)

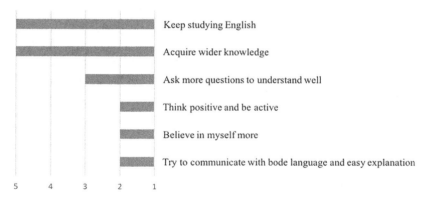

Figure 5.5 Solution to the Challenges
Source: GIC (2020)

convey your thoughts". Real and meaningful communication starts when the other receives what you want to say. In this course, by using acting training and theatre exercises, the students experienced the circulation of communication with our whole being.

(3) Dialogue: CREATOYO Global Creativity Week

The third basis for our programme is *Dialogue.* One-year study outside Japan, journeys to visit innovation hubs outside Japan, and a diverse environment where around 30% of students are international allow students to acquire the capability to take action to resolve global problems and collaborate internationally by using their dialogue skills. Innovations in a new era will be pioneered through dialogue between globally effective human capital who shares expert knowledge and skills beyond their organizational or institutional boundaries.

CREATOYO is an annual one-week interactive training aimed at apprehending creativity through a variety of contexts and experiences. The program is organized by Hajime Imamura and René Carraz of the Department of Global Innovation Studies (GINOS), in collaboration with MOSAIC, the creativity and innovation hub from HEC Montreal, Canada and BETA from Strasbourg University. During the week-long program, a blend of lectures, exhibitions, round-tables, workshops and visits of creative spaces enable the participants to gain a better grasp of what is creativity and how Tokyo, and Japan more generally, are crafting and nurturing their creative ecosystems.

On the basis of the three concepts of *Travel, Play, and Dialogue*, we intend to expand our network, favour interactions and generate opportunities for both theoretical and case-driven dialogues around creativity. By working together with local and international business leaders, civil servants, academics, creative operators, and students, the program intends to create an interactive event where we mix and remix creative ideas and concepts.

Conclusion and Future Prospects

The encounter between our new department, GINOS, and the Mondragon MTA, which occurred at an extremely serendipitous time, may prove to be historic in retrospect in terms of achieving its goal of compensating for the lack of entrepreneurship in Japan.

Japan's human resource development system, which achieved high economic growth, performed extremely well in building human capital through long-term employment and internal human resource development modelled on that of large-scale corporations. Within the pyramidal internal labour market formed by internal promotion, the systematic job rotation formed skills with many company-specific elements. This is the so-called membership type employment system.

However, with the intensification of global competition and innovation, long-term human resource development plans are no longer able to provide the necessary human resources, and an increasing number of Japanese companies have recently declared that they cannot maintain lifetime employment and are shifting from membership-based employment to job-based employment.

As the differentiation and competitiveness of everyone as a human resource is now being sought, we focused our attention on the *Teampreneur* education of the MTA, which we happened to encounter in another study meeting.

We were strongly attracted to the fact that MTA educates students to solve real-world problems by practicing business in a concrete way, and we immediately understood the need for education that aims to generate profits in the future, even though it only proposes practical solutions to problems at present.

However, there are things that can be done in Europe, such as Spain, that are too difficult to do in Japan. It is the ability to communicate freely and actively. In a governance structure that was originally accustomed to a top-down, bureaucratic decision-making system, it is not easy to create new business by collaborating across organizational boundaries. Therefore, our Travel Play Dialogue project studies course is offered as a package that includes overcoming the communication issues of Japanese people. English Communication Exercise Using Acting Training was included for this purpose.

CREATOYO is an intensive course that brings together entrepreneurs, business experts, researchers, and students to solve problems of creativity management in the innovation society and economy, and it is intended to provide an opportunity for students and companies to encounter each other in the form of actual business activities, which is critically rare in Japan.

In summary, our Travel Play Dialogue Project Studies provided a new and expanded ecosystem to achieve the educational outcomes of the MTA more effectively in the different context of Japan. In the future, it is necessary to collaborate with MTAs and other advanced case studies to strengthen the ecosystem for practicing entrepreneurship, especially around human power, which was particularly low in the GIC innovation ranking mentioned at the beginning of this report. To this end, we will continue to accumulate original research on human resource development and develop educational programs that are more suited to the Japanese context.

References

Cabinet Office. (2016). *Society 5.0.* https://www8.cao.go.jp/cstp/society5_0/index.html

GINOS(2020). *Department of Global Innovation Studies four-year process of learning.* www.toyo.ac.jp/-/media/Images/Toyo/academics/faculty/grs/dgis/114442/_p83_.ashx?la=ja-JP&hash=75EBA1819564312CDC2053636164C1C479078C65

GIC Center for Global Innovation Studies. (2018). Development of Entrepreneurship through Learning Journey. Report of Learning Journey 23rd February to 11th March in 2018, Internal research report of Center for Global Innovation Studies, Toyo University.

GIC Center for Global Innovation Studies. (2020). *Yearbook global innovation rankling 2019.* Center for Global Innovation Studies, Tokyo: Toyo University.

Japan External Trade Organization (JETRO). (2019). *JETRO Japan Investment Report 2019"—Creating Innovation through foreign capital in the region.* www.jetro.go.jp/news/releases/2019/196ec7b38c355ff3.html

Keidanren. (2018). *Society 5.0—Creating the future together.* Keidanren Policy (Proposals—Reports). www.keidanren.or.jp/policy/2018/095.html

Keizai Doyukai (Japan Association of Corporate Executives). (2015). *No expansion of investment in Japan without change in Japan: Preparedness of companies and government is the key.* www.doyukai.or.jp/policyproposals/articles/2015/150601a.html

Ministry of Economy, Trade and Industry (METI). (2018). *Global venture ecosystem collaboration enhancement project report for 2018.* Ministry of Economy, Trade and Industry (METI). www.meti.go.jp/main/yosan/yosan_fy2018/pr/ip/sansei_04.pdf

Ministry of Education, Culture, Sports, Science and Technology (MEXT). (2017). *Next generation entrepreneur development project (EDGE-NEXT).* www.mext.go.jp/a_menu/jinzai/edge/1346947.htm

Persol Research Institute. (2019). *APAC employment status and growth consciousness survey.* https://rc.persol-group.co.jp/research/activity/data/apac_2019.html

Toyo University (2016). Beyond 2020 https://www.toyo.ac.jp/en/foundation/beyond2020/

6 Challenges for the Introduction of New Teaching Methods in Brazilian Higher Education

Team Academy "Tupiniquim"

Roberta Leme Sogayar and Tomás Sparano Martins

Introduction

From the early 1950s, Brazil has been struggling to put into practice a Higher Education national learning strategy that could generate applied knowledge to promote sustainable development (De Mello et al., 2011; Maculan & De Mello, 2009). At the same time organizations have lacked the internal capacity to absorb and benefit from the knowledge generated by the universities and, as such, there has been a clear tendency to develop their own technology or obtain it externally. The connections between the universities and the private sector are still weak. Brazilian universities have initially been founded with a strong, non-flexible, traditional teaching mission, and only started incorporating entrepreneurship, innovation, and experiential learning practices by the end of the 2010s due to the pressure put by the advancement of new technologies and innovation on students and organizations (De Mello et al., 2011).

This context and the reputation of the "Finnish Education Concept", acquired mainly when Finland ranked first in the Programme for International Student Assessment (PISA) in 2001 (Schleicher, 2019), seemed the perfect scenario for Team Academy in Brazil. As a result, two young entrepreneurs Mr. Melkko and Ms. Kääriäinen from Monkey Business, developed an educational project in São Paulo based on *Tiimiakatemia* from 2009 to 2011 together with Partus Oy and Senac São Paulo (National Service of Commercial Learning). During the process in Brazil, Melkko and Kääriäinen felt that there were opportunities for TA projects based on the development of entrepreneurial skills and experiential education in both public and private Brazilian educational sectors. They also saw possibilities in private companies, so they opened a business in Brazil to explore these two markets: education and the overall private business sector. But, since

DOI: 10.4324/9781003163176-7

then, we haven't seen the development of a long-term structured applied TA endeavour in Brazil. Why?

To answer this question, we analysed the independent initiative of three Team Coaches that underwent the TA Coaching Training Program conducted by Monkey Business and Partus in 2012–2013. The three initiatives were conducted in the Brazilian Higher Education context. This chapter describes each coach's environment and the way they adapted TA's practices to overcome limitations, bureaucracy, and corporate expectations imposed by the educational system. But, before we go into that, let's take a look at the Higher Education (HE) structure in Brazil.

Modern Brazilian universities only emerged in the early 20th century, Brazilian universities are newer than those of other countries in Latin America (Leal et al., 2012). They do not align with the paths of Higher Education in Europe or the United States, although in distinct moments they have been influenced by both systems. During the 1950s to 1970s, several public universities were created in Brazil. A boost in HE took place in the 1970s driven by the depletion of public resources that led to the growth of the private sector that opened new programmes to meet the increasing HE demands. Under these circumstances, the commercialization of HE led to the offer of many programmes of questionable quality (Sogayar and Rejowski, 2014).

A further change and increase in demand occurred in the 1990s when quality HE became a basic condition for young people to succeed in their professional life. The demand for better quality led the government to develop regulatory standards and apply recurring quality assessments. As a result, the 2000s were marked by the implementation of various assessment tools and both flexibility and openness for new and alternative pedagogical approaches and delivery methods. Besides that, the pressures arising from societal issues such as sustainability, globalization, innovation, entrepreneurship, ethics, and social inclusion forced HE to incorporate these issues into their curricula. These curriculum changes and the increasing access to a range of teaching and learning technologies led students to be less willing to engage in traditional teaching ("sage on the stage") settings.

Nowadays, Brazilian HE Institutions (HEIs) struggle to keep up with changes in industry, which is demanding professionals that can adapt to diverse market conditions and employ their skills in a flexible, multifunctional way and in new fields of knowledge, organizational, and social practice (Saraiva et al., 2009). Martens and Freitas (2006) observe that, in general, HEIs traditionally prepared their students and teachers for a formal job market, which has been changing due to the dynamics of markets themselves, inserted in a dynamic, globalized economy with rapid technological advances. Besides the need for knowledge related to entrepreneurship, innovation, creativity, and interdisciplinarity, there is still a need for a continuous development of critical thinking in young adults and human skills to act in both businesses and social and environmental settings (Audy, 2017).

Besides that, HEIs face the challenge to deliver learning through experience, context, practical orientation, using information and communication technologies for the development of technical and socio-emotional skills applied to solving real-world problems. As result, HEIs are pressured to create new programmes, curricula, courses, subjects, and classes with a focus on the development of applied skills in life (Seemiller & Grace, 2017), including work and active participation as citizens of a changing society. In this new context, the purpose of the chapter is reflected on the learnings of three Brazilian cases, and discusses present and the future possibilities for TA implementation in the country. We conducted semi-structured interviews with three Brazilian coaches in three different contexts to collect data related to their TA experiences and build the cases.

Case 1 – Reflections from a Public University Perspective

Coach 1 has been working in a university environment for more than 20 years, mostly in private institutions, but only in 2013 he officially joined a public university. He never thought TA methodology would work in a private university due to the need to fulfil a full load of class hours with traditional lectures. On the other hand, in the public university, due to the openness and space, he imagined he could develop and implement a TA integral project after a self-convincing and internalization process of the TA methodology effectiveness.

However, during his first year teaching freshmen at the public university he noticed that students were not ready for a change in the teaching and learning paradigm. Students (3 classes of 50 students each) expected to sit in a chair and receive passively the knowledge they were looking for. So, he tried to adapt TA into a fixed script and label it as an entrepreneurial academic activity. Unfortunately, it did not work because he ignored the need for time and space required to develop soft skills.

As 2013 was his first year in the institution he did not want to let others think that he was not teaching (considering the teacher centred paradigm of the university). So, he tried to mix "expositive" lessons with more dialogue-oriented lessons but it also didn't work.

For his sophomore students (1 class of 30 students) he used TA modules for a specific project within a marketing course. They used several TA techniques and strategies so that in the end they would have a digital product with solid indicators. The system started to give signs of birth.

So, he developed what he calls a "Marketing Lab for value co-creation in teams", as an open and free activity, not part of the regular curriculum. That took place on Saturdays and it was very successful. Having this experience as a framework, he designed an extension programme open to the community, and some of his former students were invited to be part of the growing network that TA usually demands. But he had to deal with a great amount of bureaucracy within the university system, and he had no support for all the activities he wanted to undertake or an infrastructure that would be appealing for those who were not part of the university. He started to struggle with the fact of being "alone" in terms of being the only one working with TA methods at the institution.

In his third year at University (in his freshmen class), he went back to the lecture theatre model since he felt that this young group had concrete challenges to relate as a team. Some of these students joined his Marketing Lab, mostly because of the "word of mouth" that had the "cool" label on it.

After five years of trying different models with different groups, he put together all his learning experiences around TA and developed another extension program. This time he was counting on the support of former students (those who were familiarized with TA methods) to develop a network of TA minds. Here he had to develop booklets and learning materials to support students' development and used different spaces in town. He was not locked within the university structure. It took him five years to find a model that would converge into the Brazilian market. He noticed that if the entrepreneurship teaching model deviates from academic standards it does not survive within the HE environment.

It is not easy to be the only one in the university trained with TA methods. At first, it seemed like an advantage, but he understood the creation of an environment with actors that "speak the same language" would have been more fruitful for everyone involved. Working alone prevents the method from reaching its potential.

He needed other people so the engine would function. He tried to engage his colleagues, but disbelief was the general feeling, friendliness was non-existent, individualism was mainstream within his peers. Given that he saw this from his colleagues, he never emphasized the TA brand when discussing his ideas with them, he just felt that it was easier to communicate general ideas like a new program for "team building", "customer engagement", or "agile methods". As a result, the students never associated their training (perceived as different and innovative) with TA. He found it very hard to "sell" what TA delivers. Finally, even though the bureaucratic infrastructure of a public university is a barrier to implement innovation in general, he thinks that the individual freedom that professors have to create and design their own programmes could be a strong driver to develop an organic TA ecosystem among public universities.

Case 2 – Reflections from a Private University

Coach 2 has had her TA *teaching* experience in a private university owned by an international group of universities, strictly regulated by the government. In institutions like these, you can observe a greater number of students and teachers with a heavy teaching load, usually paid by the hour. Historically, classes have been teacher-centred but at this specific institution, there was an effort to develop active learning methodologies. This was when Coach 2 was allowed to implement part of TA methodology within the Marketing degree, focusing on their final year marketing project. This class had 40 students in total and the project was assigned only 4 hours per week, so to implement a TA culture for these students was quite challenging.

In the initial sessions (where Coach 2 was presenting TA concepts and what would be expected from them) controversy arise among some students, and 20% of the class wanted to get back to the original format of their final traditional project (classic business plan model), but the remaining of the class were excited about the challenges ahead. The class was divided into 2 teams (through Belbin's test), and they had their coaching sessions every other week.

It is important to note that this was an evening course where most students worked during the day to pay their tuition fees. Another important fact is that this profile of students was not inclined to have and share reading assignments and the initial dialogue sessions could not be supported by students' insights and contributions. Nevertheless, some of those who were more experienced workers would bring real-life experience to be shared, which demonstrated to be extremely helpful but intimating for those who were not at the same level yet.

The real challenge for Coach 2 was to deal with the criticism from the teachers of the other subjects who were not involved in the TA process and were still holding back into the old project model. For the students, their challenges (besides all of those described by Lehtonen, 2013) was to be involved in a process where the focus was not around numbers (translated into grades), but their skills, where their personal side was at stake and where they had to prove their ability to be good marketing professionals since they were seniors.

Another interesting aspect Coach 2 observed was that these seniors had been studying together for three years but they never opened themselves to interact with all their colleagues in class. So, after Belbins' test was applied and new groups were formed, there was a lot of resistance to be part of a team where they did not feel comfortable with. They were just not used to working in teams.

Besides all their challenges in terms of developing a new business idea and the question of raising money for a graduation trip, in their final evaluation they mentioned that their greatest accomplishments were on their personal development. TA project gave them the space for self-development, something that has been lacking within curriculums in Brazil.

In the second year using TA as a final project, Coach 2 implemented it on the final year of a Tourism degree and the profile of students was quite different since that was a morning class with a minority of students working full-time. They were less mature but more hands-on projects. Their willingness to travel played a great role within their motivational system and one of the teams was able to accomplish their goal by the end of two semesters.

The challenges reported by Coach 2 relate to the lack of an ecosystem that supports the development of the methodology. First is within the university itself, and second, within a business network. It is important to note, that Coach 2 had a full-time teaching position, with 32 hours of classroom, having little time to engage with business owners and organizations to seed possibilities for students. The network was formed mainly by the coach's network of former students. The lack of knowledge about TA and the lack of space to train other teachers did not promote a collaborative environment where teachers of other subjects and the Coach 2 could engage. Most teachers were sceptical and critical about what they were being offered.

But the moment of truth arrived when the first *birthgiving*[1] was presented in both programmes. Examining board members were very surprised by the visual quality and creativity of students, but mostly with the complexity of the delivered projects as well as their evidence of personal development. The second *birthgiving* of the year for both programmes (which was their final graduation project), was delivered in a complete learning experience. In both cases, students felt that they had really accomplished something different than the other students in the university and they want to "show off". As an example, one of the teams delivered a whole "Alice in the wonderland" storytelling using all TA analogies and their practical entrepreneurial examples. Visually it was very appealing and with high cognitive capacity. Examiners were very impressed, and students were deeply pleased with their accomplishments as individuals and as a group. The main complaint about the whole project was regarding the moment of its implementation. They wished TA had been a concept right from the beginning of the programme. Another restraint was the rotation system that this specific private university had as the following year, Coach 2 was teaching other subjects.

Case 3 – The Incubator in a Confessional University

Coach 3 worked in a confessional university (a religious private institution) and in 2013 she was managing one of the most solid incubators in Rio de Janeiro. She used her team coach abilities to coach the companies that were incubated (mostly students and former students). Because these students were already engaged as business starters, their level of engagement with TA methods was higher. But what worked as motivation was also a matter of disagreement when they had to change roles within the company, as they did not go through an effective process to form a team. At this incubator, they had to adjust TA methods to fit smaller teams and their needs. In a 360° evaluation,[2] they could not debate personal issues affecting their relationship as a team, but they could only focus on how the work itself was affected. They never used self-evaluation looking at their personal level development only, but how their traits could affect the business. Coach 3 recognizes it was an adjustment that had to be done so students would not criticize the incubator.

Coach 3 decided then to open a TA course for the general public within the university for those who wanted to develop their business idea throughout a year, as an elective course. Several students engaged within this course but she faced the challenges of dealing with those students who signed up thinking that they were just going to get an "easy grade". So, grading had to be extremely objective and with clear metrics (going back to the original grading method) and her work became tied to tasks to be covered rather than real business projects, team work, and personal development related reflections.

However, the programme was successful within the university environment and it was expanded as an extension activity (open to the general public). Within this model Coach 3, had to make several adaptions using her business experience because students wanted the programme to have a more well-defined structure. The dialogue coaching method and the collective construction of knowledge were elements that were challenging for groups using TA for the first time. She also suggests that a strong barrier within the implementation of TA is the rigid structure proposed by the Ministry of Education. In her opinion, TA is more a personal development methodology based on business (and other areas) advancement. She also highlights that if the student does not have a well-defined path from the beginning it is very hard for them to accomplish a whole TA process. For her specific university model, she believes TA would be a great fit for a business or marketing minor degree.

She believes that in order for TA to be implemented within a university system, these institutions would need an innovation policy to support new practices to face the fear of criticism from the Ministry of Education.

Reflections

According to what was described in the cases presented we can see that the 3 Coaches were eager to put TA into practice in their own different contexts. So, each one of them developed isolated initiatives in their HE institutions and faced several barriers (Table 6.1) to deliver the experience to their students. According to these cases, most of the impediments were related to the Brazilian HE structure, the Brazilian Social Structure, and the Scale-based Private University Business Model. As a result, they had to develop several adaptations to the TA model to overcome what was setting them back.

As each coach faced their own barriers individually, they came up with incremental solutions to adapt the methodology and deliver the program they initially created on their own. Basically, according to these experiences, they applied parts of the methodology in a way that it would fit into the HE structure, Private University Business Model, and the current Brazilian Social Structures. The adaptations ranged from including other experiential learning by doing methods, and more traditional approaches to deal with a large number of students or the lack of collective leaning/sharing

Table 6.1 Brazilian TA programme implementation barriers

Barriers	Nature
Sequential Course Structure in University Formal Programmes	HE Structure
External Quality Assessment by the Ministry of the Education based on traditional indicators	HE Structure
Traditional Grading System	HE Structure
Teacher Assessment based on traditional indicators aligned with the Ministry of Education External Assessment	HE Structure
Bureaucracy to develop new programmes	HE Structure
Instructors paid by the hour	Private University Business Model
Too many students in class	Private University Business Model and/ or Public University Inclusion System
Students have to cope with full working hours and study at the same time.	Brazilian Social Structure
Innovative Methodologies and Practices for few	Brazilian Social Structure
Lack of collective learning/sharing mindset	Brazilian Social Structure

Source: Authors' own

mindset. As a result, students that took part in the projects perceived value in TA as a change-maker experience and a way to develop their soft skills. This is of great importance as nowadays firms see soft skills as more important and relevant than hard skills for their future marketing professionals. As a result, we can see that the adaptations proposed by the coaches did not deal with the major barriers in the Brazilian HE context, but they generated high value for the participants.

The drawback of this incremental scenario proposed by the cases is that we cannot see a sustainable long-term proposal for TA in Brazil in the near future. According to the cases, in order to come up with an endeavour of such nature, a strong narrative is needed to translate the TA experience into a discourse aligned with the social challenges and paradigm shift that the Brazilian HE needs and as a revenue model for private institutions. The coaches' adaptation processes do not reveal the best way to put this long-term proposal into practice, but they suggest some possibilities: TA as an undergraduate program; TA as part of other current programmes; or, TA as an extracurricular activity.

One of the main issues identified in the cases is the fact that the three coaches work alone and have difficulties engaging peers to share and work together. In order to overcome this problem, under the new digitally transformed environment, we think the TA coaches should work closely using the global TA network to support their local initiatives.

Monkey Business trained four independent coaches in Brazil after their first project with Senac, three of them shared their experiences in the presented cases. We understand that the future of TA in Brazil depends on the building of a network of coaches and participants. However, training new coaches is very expensive especially with the current high exchange rate and overall economic situation in Brazil and existing coaches do not have the capacity to deliver that training due to time limitations. Apart from that, there are language barriers in Brazil that hinder participation in the global TA network. So, what's next? One of the main issues in the cases is that we could not see a general, clear objective for TA in Brazil. The coaches had their own objectives, adapted the model to reach them, succeed to deliver a change-maker experience for the participants, and constructed their own journey that is the Tupiniquim[3] TA model. But, it is time to envision a bigger picture and a plan to make the full TA dream in Brazil happen.

Final Considerations

Our purpose in the chapter was to propose a discussion about the present and future possibilities for TA in the Brazilian Higher Education context based on the previous experiences of three coaches. As we presented, the Brazilian HE environment is complex, highly regulated, and competitive.

Therefore, we identified several structural barriers for more sustainable initiatives based on an innovative approach like TA.

According to the cases, the coaches were able to adapt the methodology to partially deliver an entrepreneurial, relational, and reflective experience for their students. The results were considerate in terms of developing soft skills, creative thinking, and teamwork.

Having a university degree no longer guarantees a job or a career. Nowadays, we see people constantly building their professional path, it is not an end, but a means to adapt to the constant change proposed by a dynamic global context. So, it is clear that there is a need for personal and organizational knowledge related to entrepreneurship, innovation, creativity, interdisciplinarity, and critical thinking.

Brazilian HEIs will continue to struggle to help their students build their learning paths in this new context if they do not overcome some of the main HE structural barriers presented in the cases. TA is an opportunity for them to deliver learning through experience, practice, and relevance to solve real-world problems. However, as we have seen in our cases, first there is a need to build a Brazilian TA narrative to connect people and institutions within a local and global network and to "sell" the TA idea.

Notes

1 Birth giving is team's oral and/or written interactive presentation its current competency.
2 A 360-degree evaluation is a multi-source feedback process through which team members give and receive feedback and conduct their own self-evaluation.
3 In Brazil, the term "Tupiniquim" colloquially means "Brazilian" or "national".

References

Audy, J. (2017). A inovação, o desenvolvimento e o papel da Universidade. *Estudos Avançados, 31*(90), 75–87. https://doi.org/10.1590/s0103-40142017.3190005

De Mello, J. M. C., Maculan, A.-M., & Renault, T. B. (2011). Brazilian universities and their contribution to innovation and development. In *Universities in transition* (pp. 53–76). New York: Springer. https://doi.org/10.1007/978-1-4419-7509-6_4

Leal, S. R., Netto, A. P., & Trigo, L. G. G. (2012). Tourism education and research in Brazil. In *Tourism in Brazil* (pp. 199–214). Abingdon: Routledge https://doi.org/10.4324/9780203121801-19

Lehtonen, T. (2013). *Tiimiakatemia: How to grow to become a team entrepreneur.* Jyväskylä: JAMK University of Applied Sciences.

Maculan, A.-M., & de Mello, J. M. C. (2009). University start-ups for breaking lock-ins of the Brazilian economy. *Science and Public Policy, 36*(2), 109–114. https://doi.org/10.3152/030234209x406791

Melkko, V. (2012). *Brazilian educational market: Exporting Finnish educational concepts to an exotic country [Bachelor's theses]*. Jyväskylä: JAMK University of Applied Sciences.www.theseus.fi/bitstream/handle/10024/46324/Thesis-Brazilian_Educational_market_Valtteri_Melkko_May2012.pdf?sequence=1&is Allowed=y

Saraiva, L. A. S., Bauer, M. A. L., & Paiva, K. C. M. (2009). Desafios no universo das organizações de educação superior. *Revista Gestão & Planejamento, 10*(2), 179–192.

Schleicher, A. (2019). *PISA 2018: Insights and interpretations*. OECD Publishing. https://doi.org/10.1787/9789264301603-en

Seemiller, C., & Grace, M. (2017). Generation Z: Educating and engaging the next generation of students. *About Campus, 22*(3), 21–26. https://doi.org/10.1002/abc.21293

Sogayar, R. L., & Rejowski, M. (2014). Tourism, hospitality and events curriculum in higher education in Brazil: reality and challenges. In *The Routledge handbook of tourism and hospitality education* (pp. 242–256). London: Routledge. https://doi.org/10.4324/9780203763308

7 Reflections Around Team Academy Inspired Projects in Argentina

Natalia Ceruti

How the Story Started

It was April 2009 when I first stepped into the famous *Tiimiakatemia* premises, in Jyväskylä, Finland. I was supposed to visit the *Centre of Excellence in Entrepreneurship*. I was not very fond of the idea: in my home university, being an entrepreneur meant that you could basically write a Business Plan and pitch it to win an entrepreneurial contest. Nothing else. No real business just talks and rhetoric. Having that in mind, my prejudice was that I was going to meet a bunch of students who were eager to show off ideas that would never come to life. Oh, my goodness, how far was I from that! Fortunately, I was an exotic visitor and thus my presence at *Tiimiakatemia* was required, despite of my reluctancy to go. I will never ever forget that first step into Team Academy (TA). It was as if a rush of energy had invaded me through the bones.

Nowadays, we are used to co-working spaces, and the *Google-office-style* has almost become a standard. Back in 2009, all you could expect at a university was to see classrooms with students staring at each other´s necks. You can certainly imagine how that first glimpse of *Tiimiakatemia* was as shocking as refreshing. I spent several days with the Team Coaches and Team Entrepreneurs in order to learn more about this process of learning with no classes and no exams. I fell in love with the concept, and obviously imagined plenty of *Tiimiakatemias* being implemented in Latin America. I made it my own entrepreneurial quest. I do not have proper statistics to back it up, but I can assure that is certainly the most frequent reaction visitors have.

At that time, I was mainly interested in bringing a radical method to this other part of the world. Tiimiakatemia appeared to be a well-structured way of doing things differently. I liked some parts of the method because I already had the intuition that *learning by doing* was a better way of learning to do business, and some other parts they simply blew my mind. And

DOI: 10.4324/9781003163176-8

so, I started my own learning process. As a licensed business administrator, I felt Tiimiakatemia was much more than simply a way to learn business. I attended the Team Mastery program and I strongly felt it all had more to do with the learning process itself than with the business topics. I needed to know more in order to decipher the magic. I enrolled for a second degree as a Psychologist, as well as a Master in Cognitive Psychology and Learning. If there's something Tiimiakatemia triggered, that was the opening of a path of new discoveries and self-transformation. I will never be grateful enough for that.

Becoming an Educational Entrepreneur

The plan was alive and kicking: we would have (at least) one *Tiimiakatemia* per country, in Latin America, by 2020.

The process included two main steps: (1) Learning more about TA and related ideas and (2) Finding implementation partners and/or investors. And it all had to be done in a sustainable way (a.k.a. earning money to live!).

The first part of the plan was successfully fulfilled. Not only with formal learning, but also with non-mainstream courses in topics such as Art of Hosting, Appreciative Inquiry, Graphic Facilitation, Spiral Dynamics, U Theory, and many others. Also, as I wanted to understand how *Tiimiakatemia* had developed outside Finland. I visited The Netherlands, the Basque Country, and the UK. I travelled plenty, and I personally met incredible people such as Peter Senge, Otto Scharmer, Don Beck, Pablo Villoch, Juliana Almeida Dutra, Cecilia Soriano, Martín Castro, Pauline Van der Pas, Alison Fletcher, and many others, from whom I learnt much more than mere tools and methods. As for the personal sustainability side, this part was clearly an investment.

The second part was not so linear as our overly excited entrepreneurial minds tend to think when embarking in a new project. I strongly felt I had to make a university from scratch. But still I decided to reach out to one of the most important private universities in Argentina. It is known to be *the university for entrepreneurs.* I was supported by Andy Freire, our local Jeff Bezos of that time. He loved the idea and was a former student. What could go wrong? Well, as for a full response, the Rector (Dean) told me: *I like it, but it is too innovative. We are fine as we are* (personal communication, 7th December, 2013). We all know the road of entrepreneurs is paved with frustration, but still, it hurts when it happens.

After this drawback I decided I would not contact any other local university. My first impression was confirmed: they cannot even start to grasp the idea. I lately understood that, in those countries where *Tiimiakatemia* was implemented successfully inside universities, there is at least one of the main components of the method that they already understand and value: co-operation in the Basque country and coaching in the UK. None of those ideas are present in our local universities, so there was nothing to piggy-back on. It's definitely too radical even nowadays.

One of the metrics I adore about *Tiimiakatemia* is the one that states you need to fulfil a certain amount of Customer Visits within a given period of time. It has proven to be one of the best tools for my own entrepreneurial quest. Each time I visited someone I learned more and more about the project and how to improve it. But if there's one visit that truly paid off, that was the one to Andy Freire. Not only did he connect me to the university, but he also provided feedback on the project and even opened up the option of implementing the idea in parts. I would be lying if I said I accepted the challenge immediately: I was in love with the pure concept of having a radical new way of learning (building included) that the sole idea of breaking it in parts sounded as a crime. But sustainability brought me down to earth very quickly!

Andy connected me with Mercedes Miguel (now, my friend *Mechi*). She was in charge of the planning area of the Ministry of Education of the City of Buenos Aires. At that time, she was in charge of leading a major transfor-mation in the secondary school curriculum. In Argentina, attending second-ary school is compulsory and includes education from ages 13 to 17. Yes, teenagers.

Introducing an educational reform is never an easy task. Even more in a jurisdiction with more than 700 schools (private and public) and 18 highly-politicized teacher unions. When I met Mercedes for the first time, she was interested in the Finnish Model of education for primary schools (ages 6 to 12). But after some minutes of talking, it became evident that her most chal-lenging task was to transform the outdated secondary school into the *Nueva Escuela Secundaria* (New Secondary School, which meant re-designing not only the curriculum but also the teaching practices). She was full of energy and passionate about the challenge. She was also surprisingly open to radi-cal ideas. She was different. And that was a good thing.

The year before meeting Mercedes I had run my first *Tiimiakatemia* pilot. It was a programme called *Jump Lab*. Carlos Miceli, a local entrepreneur had put together a series of tools and interviews in order to help other entre-preneurs become more successful. Back then he was already a true influ-encer for the entrepreneurial tribe. He was very well connected and so he could easily get the local entrepreneurial stars to come and have a session with us. When I saw the plan, I immediately told him: *Hey, this content is great, why don't we deliver it in a Tiimiakatemia way?* As he accepted, I flipped around all his ideas and turned the typical 8-session course into a 2-month life experience. We had 24 entrepreneurs attending the programme that was held every 2 weeks, from Thursday to Saturday, full days. Only that time-design was already highly innovative in our market. I remember we strongly had to explain the attendants they were not going to have classes the whole time! We put the participants to work in teams, we made them reflect and be accountable for themselves as well as for the team, and we finished with proper *Birth Giving*[1] sessions. Looking backwards, of course I would now do some things differently, but that was a very decent first trial of implementing something in a *Tiimiakatemia* style.

So, when Mercedes was describing the conflictive situation between students, teachers, principals, and the Ministry around the *New Secondary School*, I immediately connected with the idea around the need for more entrepreneurial spirit within the educational system. One of the main struggles to generate change was that none of the parts involved had a collaborative attitude, nor real ways to experience it or learn it. Suddenly, all the pieces connected, and I offered Mercedes a similar kind of *Jump Lab* program for *educational actors.*

Creating *Emprendizaje*

Mercedes was not very sure of what I would do, but she is was brave and courageous (or was so desperate!), that she gave me a go to start a programme with teachers.

An Argentine, they say, is an Italian who speaks Spanish but thinks he is English. I believe it´s quite an accurate way to describe our culture. How could I then design a process, keeping the so Finnish *Tiimiakatemia* principles, for Argentinian teachers? Is there a more radical difference than the one between the Finnish and the Argentinian cultures? I was completely convinced that the essence of *Tiimiakatemia* was built around the human nature and not the culture. And this was my chance to prove it. *Jump Lab* had been successful, but they were all self-motivated millennial entrepreneurs. How could I work with disappointed, angry, middle aged teachers? I loved the challenge!

I named the program *Emprendizaje*, which is the conjunction of the Spanish words *Emprendimiento* (entrepreneurship) and *Aprendizaje* (learning). The idea was that you, as a teacher, could be an entrepreneur of your own learning, and also facilitate the learning of others in an entrepreneurial way.

Emprendizaje was the cornerstone of a more ambitious project. The idea was to create *Emprendizaje* Units (similar to *Tiimiakatemia hubs*) inside every public school in Buenos Aires. In order to achieve that goal, the first step was to make the teachers go through the experience as learners (*Emprendizaje*), then learn how to facilitate *Emprendizaje* programmes, and ultimately, create, support, and develop those *Emprendizaje* Units as part of an *Emprendizaje* Network.

The first thing I did was to improve the *Jump Lab* design and made it be more suitable for the teachers. For the new participants, the purpose was not to start a business project, but to create a great learning environment. It took me almost 6 months to convince Mercedes that the programme could not be compulsory but rather an opportunity for the teachers to freely join.[2] Another disruption for the system was that it was not going to be held in the typical class format (maximum 4 hours per day, twice a week), but in an intensive an immersive way (4 modules of 2 and half days per module), outside the school, in rented ball rooms in a centric hotel. I could write a new article only describing all the bureaucratic processes we had to comply with (or finally avoid) in order to have those teachers coming to *Emprendizaje*'s first edition.

I used a very different way to promote the programme. I did not publish the typical ad stating contents, workload, and points to be granted,[3] but instead I published a colourful Ad claiming: *Do you enjoy challenges? Are you inspired to be part of change? Do you consider yourself an entrepreneur?* I clearly stated it was going to be held during long days, and that it would not give the participants any points. I tried to be as discouraging as possible. I had very few spots, and I only wanted the really motivated teachers to come.

The plan worked well. Putting a great effort, and after 3 months of promotion, I got 29 amazing participants to be seated in our first circle. The main takeout of that first check-in was that they had no idea why they were there, but that they just felt they wanted to come. Great start, indeed.

The modules were designed to start with very deep self-reflections, then move to expectations about educational settings, and finally create real actions/artefacts to make the changes come to life. I introduced several business concepts[4] that could be used for school projects, and all learning was achieved by doing (projects) in teams. The participants were thrilled about the experience and most of them described the programme as life-changing.

With that single *Emprendizaje* edition I learned that, even though the system was shaking, some teachers were eager to reconnect with their own love for learning and use it as a platform to catalyse change. So, I it was clear that I had to facilitate a second edition.

Word of mouth is powerful, and mostly among teachers. The very first day I published the opening of a new programme, all the spots were taken. *Emprendizaje* had 6 editions, distributed along 3 years. Each time I needed to add more and more *obstacles* in order to get the most motivated candidates. For the last edition, I told them they even had to find a place for us to meet and come on Saturdays. Still, I got more than 200 applications for 40 spots.

After the second edition, Mercedes asked me to implement *Emprendizaje* for Principals and Supervisors.[5] It was called *Participatory Leadership Programme*. It was shorter, but it had the same essence. It was ok, but not that passionate. In the end, we all understood it would work better if we could mix all the actors. It took some time, but after the third edition, all *Emprendizaje* programmes were held including teachers of all levels, principals, supervisors and, sometimes, students.

Emprendizaje finished as soon as Mercedes got out from office. It is a tradition in Argentina to block, neglect, deny or destroy what a previous politician had made.

We could never finish the big plan: those *Emprendizaje* Units were never built in the City of Buenos Aires. What we could achieve was to build the Network. Every time an *Emprendizaje* edition ended, we invited the old *Emprendizajeros* (that's how Emprendizaje attendants call themselves) to come to the closing ceremony. We fostered a couple of *Emprendizaje* events where they could share their new practices. The community grew strong. It was amazing to witness how they kept the collaborative spirit alive. They were helping each other even if they were from different schools. That was something completely impossible to see before *Emprendizaje*. A great number of *Emprendizajeros* are now working in influential positions at different Ministries of Education or just (and not less important), changing the way students learn from their own classrooms. I always recall the cases of Leticia, who dared mixing her chemistry classes with art, or Andrea, who became an extraordinary robotics facilitator, and teacher trainer.

Going Nationwide

When Mercedes finished her time in office at the City of Buenos Aires, she became Secretary of Innovation at the National Ministry of Education. Bad news for *Emprendizaje* at Buenos Aires City level, but great news for the rest of the country.

We implemented an *Emprendizaje* version in Tucumán. Tucumán is a little province, located at the northwest side of Argentina. In general terms, the population tends to be poor, with a predominance of rural areas.

This time I could make *Emprendizaje* be even better. We planned for a process which included 3-day retreats, to be held along 2 months. We stayed in nature, and we enjoyed our human nature even more than in previous editions.

Tamara, one of the participants of the first edition of *Emprendizaje* had become a very skilled visual facilitator and a perfect assistant for the process. She was a great co-equipper from edition 2 onwards and was also key in the Tucumán edition.

The reality in an Argentinian province is very different from the reality in Buenos Aires City (the nation's capital city). If teachers in Buenos Aires enjoyed *Emprendizaje*, then those in Tucumán became fans. They were getting so little training, that when something like *Emprendizaje* arrived, it completely blew their minds.

We learned so much from the Tucumán experience. We understood that most of the principles of learning "by doing, collaborating, and working in teams" were already present, naturally, in the rural schools. This confirmed, once again, that the *Tiimiakatemia*'s essence goes straight to the human core, despite of the culture.

We had only one edition in Tucumán. But the seeds that were planted are growing very strong. Estrella, Eli, Angélica, Ceci, and Nora didn't know each other before *Emprendizaje*. During the process, they created a team that today, almost 4 years later, still works as a proper learning team. Not only have they impacted their schools, but they have also been crucial in developing and implementing creative solutions for the COVID-19 crisis.

As *Emprendizaje* was a *heavy* process[6] to implement nationwide, Mercedes wanted to have a *lighter* version that could reach more teachers. My first reaction was to get angry. How on earth could we possibly cut the process even more, and still keep the essence? It was not possible. Learning takes time, I thought.

As I could not still have my own university, nor find investors to build it, sustainability made me re-think my ideas again. Maybe there was a way to design a process that could have at least some of the essence and be delivered to plenty of people at the same time. Like a festival. The Lollapaloosa of learning. And we called it *Experiencia Aprendizaje*, which means *experience learning*.

After heavy thinking, I came to the conclusion that, at least for me, the undeniable essence of *Tiimiakatemia* is that it fosters the love for learning by providing hands on activities. It hurt in the beginning, but then I made peace with the idea that we could still have the essence while taking the team component away. It's a compromising scenario that works quite well.

Experiencia Aprendizaje was designed as a 2-day learning festival. The concept was that participants would have the time and space to experience 4 different methods/ideas, and reflect about their learning and how to put those into action.

We created a team of 15 incredible facilitators, who designed and catalysed workshops throughout the 9 editions we made. We visited a different province every month, and like the Rolling Stones, we gigged for an average of 1,500 teachers simultaneously. The idea was that participants could choose which 4 topics they preferred amongst a list of 8 different ones. We started altogether in a common area, we planned for the day, and then we got together again to touch base and trigger reflection on the learnings. It was not a deep process, but was certainly appreciated as water in the dessert by those enthusiastic teachers that attended the different editions.

The Seeds

This quote really represents the feeling I have about what we did with TA: *Don't judge each day by the harvest you reap but by the seeds that you Plant* (attributed to Robert Louis Stevenson, in Snyder, 1990, p. 148). So clear, so simple, so humble, so powerful.

The great driver was to build *Tiimiakatemias* in Latin America. That has not happened, yet. Anyhow, looking at my more than 10 years relationship with *Tiimiakatemia*, I can reflect that, in the quest for implementing an existing model I have learned and developed plenty of skills. The original motivation for bringing *Tiimiakatemia* to Argentina was that I saw it as a point of leverage to change de educational system. Maybe that is being accomplished even without the full version.

If you are reading this because you are interested in implementing *Tiimiakatemia*, please remember sometimes the context is not ready to receive and nurture ideas like *Tiimiakatemia*. But you can still proudly plant the seeds.

Notes

1 Birth Giving refers to a core *Tiimiakatemia* practice where learners bring to life a project/ idea/ artefact after a certain period of learning.
2 The traditional way of training teachers in the City of Buenos Aires is by having them to attend compulsory programmes.
3 There is a credit system that grants you *points* for attending courses. Those points are the ones you need to collect in order to advance your teaching career. It is very likely that some teachers just attend courses to get points.
4 In Argentina, there is great rejection in the educational world to bring in business concepts. They never like to see schools as organizations or companies.
5 Supervisors are the highest ranked personnel in the educational system (not including the politically appointed staff).
6 It meant at least 4 months process, trips, hotels, 12 days with teachers and principals out from school, and only for 40 participants.

Reference

Snyder, E. (1990). *Persuasive business speaking*. New York: American Management Association.

8 Adapting the Team Academy Model in a Developing Country Context

A Case of Team Entrepreneurship Education at the University of Iringa, Tanzania

Deo Sabokwigina

Introduction

This chapter reports on the efforts by the University of Iringa to implement the Bachelor of Applied Marketing and Entrepreneurship (BAME) which uses the Team Academy learning philosophy. The University introduced the BAME program in 2014/15, becoming the first University to adapt the Team Academy model in Tanzania and in Africa. The Team Academy model was developed in 1993 in Jyväskylä, Finland. At the core of the Team Academy model, there are students who work as entrepreneurs while starting and running their own enterprises as part of their studies. This model has spread to many other countries in Europe, America, Asia, and Africa. This chapter shows how the programme was introduced, how it has evolved and the challenges and opportunities therein.

The University of Iringa in a Nutshell

The University of Iringa (UoI) is the first private University to be established in Tanzania. It was established in 1993/94 and is owned by the Evangelical Lutheran Church of Tanzania through the Iringa Diocese. The University started as Iringa University College of Tumaini University until 2013 when it became a fully-fledged University with the new name of University of Iringa.

Currently, the University of Iringa has six faculties, namely, Faculty of Theology, Faculty of Arts and Social Sciences, Faculty of Science and Education, Faculty of Business and Economics, Faculty of Law and Faculty of Counselling and Psychology. Under these faculties, the Universities run a number of undergraduate and postgraduate programmes, including the Bachelor of Applied Marketing and Entrepreneurship (BAME).

DOI: 10.4324/9781003163176-9

Experience of Entrepreneurial Teaching and Learning from University of Iringa

Genesis of Entrepreneurial Teaching and Learning at the University of Iringa

A study by this chapter's author investigated the state of development of entrepreneurship education in Tanzania business schools in 2008. The study findings revealed that most entrepreneurship courses were focused on teaching students about entrepreneurship and its role in economic development. One of the study recommendations was that entrepreneurship education in Tanzania should integrate experiential learning and innovative techniques in the teaching and assessment methods (Olomi & Sabokwigina, 2010). However, by that time, the author did not fully understand how to make the course experiential and innovative.

After graduation, the author went back to the University of Iringa in 2008 and immediately was part of the founding team of the newly formed Centre for Entrepreneurship and Innovation (CEI) at the University. The Centre was tasked to mainstream entrepreneurship in curricula, conduct entrepreneurship awareness and training to students, staff, and the community; undertake entrepreneurship and business training, research and consultancy; and foster strategic partnership between the University and Industry (Chachage et al., 2021).

Through CEI, entrepreneurship got considerable promotion at the University, and in 2011, the University of Iringa updated its logo and vision to reflect the entrepreneurial orientation that the University was taking. The University indicated that its emphasis was focused on Research, Knowledge and Entrepreneurship instead of just focusing on teaching, research and consultancy. The University's vision became *to become an innovative, world class and self-sustaining University that produces ethical and entrepreneurial leaders that are capable of responding to national, regional and global challenges*. Such a vision sets a direction and commitment for transformation towards an entrepreneurial oriented University.

Despite all those efforts, we at the Centre still did not have a full picture as to how to provide an entrepreneurship education that truly generates job creators instead of job seekers. Although we knew that there had to be a shift in the way entrepreneurship education is organized and facilitated, making this shift happen in practice was a hard thing to do.

However, in 2012/2013, our entrepreneurship efforts gained more momentum after starting a cooperation with the TANZICT project, which was a Finnish funded project based at the Commission for Science and Technology (COSTECH) in Dar es Salaam. This cooperation focused on creating an entrepreneurial environment at the University whereby it is possible to foster students' entrepreneurial mindset, behaviour, and practices. Activities under this collaboration included coaching academic staff in entrepreneurial teaching and learning, raising awareness among students, exposure visit to Finland, and curriculum development.

Coaching Academic Staff in Entrepreneurial Teaching and Learning

The University of Iringa established a series of staff coaching and mentoring workshops and seminars in order to gain the staff buy-in for the entrepreneurial teaching and learning. The goal of the workshops was to raise awareness and generate ideas on new ways of teaching, mainstreaming entrepreneurship education in all programmes, and come up with new ways for linking up and serving the surrounding society and industry. The workshops were facilitated by experts from TANZICT project as well as our own staff from the Centre for Entrepreneurship and Innovation (CEI).

Raising Awareness Among Students and Staff

In 2013, the University started organizing an entrepreneurship week aimed at exposing staff and students to the world of entrepreneurship through training and testimonials, inspiration, and showcase of entrepreneurial activities/products and talents. Activities during the week intended to enhance staff and students' entrepreneurial attitudes and enable them to practice and effectively promote entrepreneurship behaviour to themselves and their surroundings. Exhibitions during the week provide an opportunity for our students who are already practising entrepreneurship or intending to start to showcase their products, services, and ideas to a bigger audience. Companies/ organizations outside the University also join in the exhibitions. The objectives of the entrepreneurship and exhibitions week are as follows:

(i)   To expose students and staff to the world of entrepreneurship through coaching and testimonials;

(ii) To inspire students and staff to develop an entrepreneurial mind-set;

(iii) To give students an opportunity to showcase their entrepreneurial activities/products and talents through exhibitions;

(iv) To collaborate with the industry in exhibitions and to give students an opportunity to interact with practitioners; and

(v) To mark the beginning of implementation of new entrepreneurial thinking at the University.

Exposure Visit to Finland

In November 2013, two CEI staff took part in a knowledge exchange and collaboration trip to Finland. They were part of a delegation comprised of representatives from five academic institutions in Tanzania. The goal of the trip was to initiate partnerships and collaboration between Tanzanian and Finnish Universities along the areas of entrepreneurship, innovation, and information technology (Sabokwigina & Mpogole, 2013)

The delegation visited many institutions. However, even before the study tour, CEI staff had already heard about Tiimiakatemia model from Finland from the TANZICT experts albeit with very few details. As such, their objectives were twofold. First, to learn the experiential learning approach used by Tiimiakatemia in developing entrepreneurial students. Second, to explore avenues for collaboration with Finnish Universities in areas of entrepreneurship and innovation (Sabokwigina & Mpogole, 2013).

The delegates learned many things during the trip including the Team Academy concept, human centred technologies, frugal innovation, incubation, co-creation, promoting innovation, models of commercialization of innovations, funding start-ups, etc. (Sabokwigina & Mpogole, 2013).

Although many areas were visited and many concepts learned, the CEI team's focus was solely on learning about the Team Academy learning philosophy. Day three of the study tour started with a visit to Tiimiakatemia of JAMK University of Applied Sciences. Students walked us around and presented to us what Tiimiakatemia is and how the model works. Those students shared their stories about their team companies and everything was truly fascinating. Also, the delegation attended a 24-hour Innovation Challenge presentation by finalist students. Even though the presentation was done in Finnish language, we could see that the presenters were able to solve the problems given to them by the external organizations and we could also appreciate the confidence of the students in their presentation (Sabokwigina & Mpogole, 2013).

Curriculum Development

Immediately after returning from Finland, a core team of five individuals was formed. The team was tasked to develop the curriculum for the

Bachelor of Applied Marketing and Entrepreneurship (BAME) which would use the Team Academy learning philosophy. The process of developing the curriculum started in early 2014 and took 1.5 years to complete it. The curriculum was vetted and approved by the Tanzania Commission for Universities (TCU) in 2015. Some of the questions that we asked ourselves during the development of the curriculum were as follows:

- What will be the output of the BAME program, i.e. what does a recent BAME graduate knows and can do?
- What is the rationale for the BAME program, i.e. why do we consider this program important?
- What are the competences that our graduates will have and what are the levels of development in different competences?
- How do our students (team entrepreneurs) acquire the competences and attitudes?

  o What courses will we have?
  o What approach and learning tools will we use in the courses?

- How do we assess the learning in this program?
- What kind of assignments should we have in this program?
- What educational environment or climate should be fostered?

Rationale of Development of BAME Programme

Youth employment continues to be one of the greatest challenges that the world faces (ILO, 2013). In Africa, the continent is estimated to have about 200 million young people aged between 15 and 24 years and the figure is expected to double in 2045 (AfDB, OECD, UNDP, UNECA, 2012). Majority of these youth will graduate from schools and Higher Education Institutions (HEIs) to start seeking for employment in the labour market. This situation reveals a "youth bulge" that calls for aggressive employment creation strategies and programmes (ILO, 2013).

In Tanzania, over 800,000 young Tanzanians leave schools and colleges every year, but less than 10% of these find employment in the formal sector (World Bank, 2014). The rest have either to remain unemployed or to create small business. Those who choose to create businesses face many barriers. They have limited knowledge, skills, and experience in starting and operating a business. Most young people are unaware of how to creatively start businesses using the opportunities around. And, those who start a business fail too often—as the so-called *death rate of start-up companies* is very high because of limited business knowledge, expertise, or experience.

There has been a major outcry from employers in Tanzania that University graduates have only knowledge but they don't possess skills and competences that employers are looking for. As a result, many graduates are unable to secure jobs in the corporate world. For example, in 2014, the Tanzania Immigration Department wanted to employ 70 new candidates but 10,816 job seekers applied for the posts (MHA, 2014). In 2017, the Tanzania Revenue Authority (TRA) advertised 400 vacancies but 56,000 Tanzanians applied for the 400 vacancies (Kimelemeta, 2017). Although these two incidents are just two high-profile cases, they tell much about the imbalance of demand for work and the availability of jobs. Indeed, producing competent entrepreneurial university graduates has always been a challenge (Mwasalwiba et al., 2012)

The pace of today's working markets is faster than before with the rapid development of Tanzanian society and information technology. Graduates must have attitudes and capabilities to adapt to these changes. Thus, education institutions should not only have a strong emphasis on educating the students about study subjects but also provide them high levels of learning to learn skills (*meta-learning* skills). A graduate who has these skills can adapt better to new situations and has the capability to learn new skills in different kind of environments. BAME places a strong emphasis on the development of individual's learning to learn skills. For example, the theory programme used in BAME programme allows the student to choose the books he/she needs for each course. This practice promotes *culture of reading* and culture of self-development.

Some lower middle-class or poor people in Tanzanian society still lack means to pay for their children's education. One solution to this is having the students work as entrepreneurs during the study time, not just after it. This practice might be able to alleviate some of the problems concerning the tuition fees. In BAME, all of the students have the possibility to operate as entrepreneurs and earn money to pay their tuitions if they need to.

Nowadays, holding degree certificates is not enough and might not act as sufficient proofs of competency to the employers of the future (Bangu et al., 2013). Employers want to see evidence of individual's real-life competency. The degree is just a minimum standard and starting point for employers. Educational institutions need to provide students real-life experiences that can be shown as evidence of one's real-life competency. A student who graduates from a university should have the degree as well as a CV with a list of real-life projects and job assignments to prove his competency. BAME as a program meets both of these requirements with a degree and evidence of real-life work experience of individuals own competencies.

Influences on BAME Learning Approaches

BAME's learning approach has influences from various approaches, models, ways of thinking and theories such as socio-constructivism, learning by doing, exploratory learning, action learning, team learning, self-managed learning, dialogue, team coaching and facilitation, team development, learning organizations and systems thinking, entrepreneurship education and entrepreneurship as holistic practice, management mindset, values, principles and tasks, Bloom's taxonomy, as well as the Knowledge-Creation Model (Nonaka & Takeuchi, 1995; Isaacs, 1999; Downey, 2003; Marquart, 2004; Katzenbach & Smith, 2006; Senge, 2006).

BAME Unique Benefits

The Bachelor of Applied Marketing and Entrepreneurship (BAME) provides the students with unique competitive edge in the work markets and sets them apart from other students who have graduated from other programmes of the same level. No other university programme in East Africa provides this much competency in these *edge areas.* These competitive edges are:

High-level of teamwork and team learning know-how both in theory and in practice. All of the students are engaged in intensive team training during the three years of study in the BAME Programme.

Developed entrepreneurial and intrapreneurial attitudes. The students get real-life experience on establishing and running a real-life business. Thus, the graduates of the programme have extra three years of experience in running a small business that other students from same level do not have. This experience develops the students' entrepreneurial attitudes and identity both on theoretical and a practical level.

Contacts to the economic life. During the study period each student develops his or her professional network. Each student has a basic network of working life contacts when he or she graduates. This increases the possibilities of employment or conducting business after the graduation.

Meta-learning skills. As the BAME learning approach is open and flexible, the students have medium- to high-level competency in self-development and attitudes in life-long learning. No other university programme in East Africa provides so many opportunities to make personal decisions, plan one's own learning and carry out self-development activities than BAME.

Modes of Delivery

BAME uses a mixed delivery style that deploys a blended learning approach. The main delivery methods include training sessions and other similar sessions with an instructor (team coach) present in the role of a guide, facilitator, and expert; independent theory studies by reading books and writing reflective book essays and other documents; and Practical learning (*Learning by Doing)* by conducting real-life projects for customers and society.

The delivery methods are linked together and need to be done parallel to each other in order to have efficient learning in BAME as indicated in Table 8.1:

Table 8.1 Links between main learning processes

	To Team Learning	To Theory Programme	To Learning by Doing
From Team Learning	–	The ideas gained from other team members are reflected upon in theory program's essays (book essays; transforming others' experiences to models and explicit knowledge)	The ideas gained from other team members are used in learning by doing activities
From Theory Program	The ideas gained from theory programme are discussed in team learning settings (sharing knowledge, peer learning from theory)	–	The theoretical models and ideas are applied to learning by doing settings (applying theory to practice; transforming explicit knowledge to tacit knowledge)
From Learning by Doing	The experiences gained from learning by doing settings are discussed in team learning settings (sharing experiences, peer learning from experiences)	The experiences gained from learning by doing (i.e. practice) are reflected upon in theory programme's documents (book essays; transforming practical experiences to models and explicit knowledge)	–

Source: Author

Learning Paths (Students' Development Levels)

As students pursue the degree of Bachelor of Applied Marketing and Entrepreneurship (BAME), they go through a learning path, during which they acquire the knowledge, skills, and practical experience necessary to develop an entrepreneurial attitude and marketing skills that will enable them to start and run their own businesses or become productive employees in an established organization. This learning path can be described as the *path of development or professional identity and capability* as shown in Table 8.2:

Table 8.2 Entrepreneurial identity development phases and challenges

Development Level	Semester in BAME	Key Challenges Faced by the Student	Team Coach's Role
Observer and Explorer	1st	Orientation to the education environment; Understanding basics of learning in a new way (meta-learning); Becoming part of the team (socialization process starts); Defining learning goals for first time; Understanding his role and the role of the teacher (team coach); First tiny projects	Guide, instructor
Experimenter	2nd	First contacts to the economic life; First projects with more responsibility; Facing the first conflicts; Defining his role and the role of the leaders (first steps of leadership development); First attempts to understand the link between theory and practice	Guide, motivator (to help the student to experiment)
Generalist	3rd	Solving team conflicts; First leadership positions; Taking more responsibility and first steps of letting go of coach as the ultimate authority; Setting more reasonable goals for learning and entrepreneurship activities	Facilitator
Specialist	4th	Choosing one's speciality field; Understanding more complex theories; Major projects (for some students); Choosing a sub-community within the wider program community (core peer group)	Facilitator, advisor
Prototyper	5th	Defining moment (commitment stage); contemplating employment (self or employed); Thinking about future; Making plans for future business (some students); Creating products or services that might be sustainably commercial	Advisor

(Continued)

Table 8.2 (Continued)

Development Level	Semester in BAME	Key Challenges Faced by the Student	Team Coach's Role
Start-Up Entrepreneur (mature entrepreneur in the context of education)	6th	Bachelor's Thesis; Realizing the first steps of future plans (trying to get employed or start a start-up business); Letting go of the safety of university and peers (saying good-byes; emotional process)	Consultant (will only give advice when asked); Research mentor

Source: Author's own

Assessment in BAME Programme

Assessment in BAME is done both *formatively* and *summatively*. *Formative assessment* is done during everyday activities by having non-formal discussions with the students. This activity is called *individual coaching* or *one-on-one coaching* where the instructor (team coach) provides the student feedback by using questions that guides the student to examine his/her learning and level of competence. In Training Sessions, the instructor (team coach) provides both the student team (*collective assessment*) as well as the individual formative assessment by asking questions and providing feedback. The team coaches also do formative assessment by providing the students written feedback notes and development ideas by writing them on students' written documents (specifically book essays, reflection chapters, and special assignments).

Formative assessment is also done in formal *Individual Development Discussions* (IDD) that is held twice a year, once per semester per student (1–2 hours per discussion). During these discussions both the student and the teacher (team coach) have the possibility of asking and giving feedback in an open-ended way that is conductive to learning and provides the team coach the opportunity to use learner-centric teaching approaches.

Summative assessment is done for each course. It is divided into continuous assessment (C) and to final assessment (F). The Tanzania Commission for Universities requires that continuous assessment should be made of assignments, tests, and quizzes. In order to meet TCU requirements, BAME's tests comprise problem solving questions and the book essays that the students write on the books they have read and that are related to the course's learning goals. On the other hand, the assignments are made of the reflection chapters that the students write for each course.

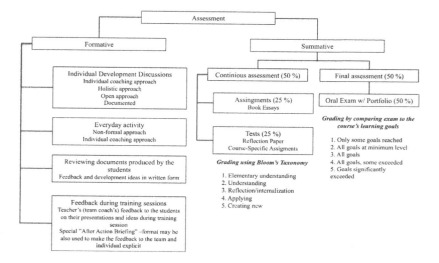

Figure 8.1 Main Features and Branches of Assessment in BAME

Source: Author's own

The final assessment is made of a Reflective Exam that is done by the student for each course. The Reflective Exams are held at end of each academic semester. The Reflective Exam is based on *course reflection and critical thinking, problem solving and performance appraisal* or *competency demonstration* focusing on knowledge, skills and competences. Before sitting for reflective exams, a student must give to the coach his or her portfolio file with documents that demonstrate his or her competency in a written form. The portfolio file consists of a training diary, learning contracts, a summary list of books read, essays written, reading plan, a summary list of projects completed, project reports, plan of making one's bachelor's dissertation, list of customers and network analysis, leadership training plan, analysis of one's learning path in general, and CV.

Preliminary Results/Impact

Students' Intake into the BAME Programme

So far, 166 students have already joined BAME programme since 2014/15 as indicated in Table 8.3. Out of the 166 students, 68 are female,

Table 8.3 BAME students' intake

	2014/15	2015/16	2016/17	2017/18	2018/19	2019/20	2020/21	Total
Male	13	5	7	2	12	20	39	98
Female	10	5	4	5	8	10	26	68
Total	**23**	**10**	**11**	**7**	**20**	**30**	**65**	**166**

Source: Author's own

constituting 41% of the total students' intake since the start of the BAME programme.

While the percentage of female students in the BAME Programme keeps fluctuating each year, we make deliberate efforts to encourage female students to join the programme, especially during the marketing campaigns of the University academic programmes. This is also emphasized in the University Gender Policy, which states that the female population recruited each year should be at least 40% of the total students admitted.

The trend in students' enrolment in the BAME Programme indicates a downward trend in enrolment from 2014/15 to 2017/18. Afterwards, there has been an upward tick in students' enrolment. This can be explained by the fact that many stakeholders are increasing becoming aware of the existence and impact of the BAME programme. However, we are currently discussing the possibility of limiting the students' intake into BAME; indeed, we have learned that it is difficult to apply Team Academy processes in large teams.

Graduation Outcomes

The first batch graduated in December 2017. Since then, we have a habit of calling our graduates six months after graduation to inquire about how they are doing and what they are doing. So far, results indicate that, six months after graduation, all graduates have jobs (60%–70% in formal jobs while 30%–40% are employed in their own enterprises).

Recognitions

In 2014, we were invited to share our experiences with other universities at the National Higher Education Forum in Arusha. In 2017, the author of this chapter was selected as part of four consultants who developed the National Framework for Integrating Enterprise Education in Teacher Training for the Ministry of Education, Science, Technology and Vocational Training (MoEST)

On 1 June 2019, the Minister of Education, Science, Technology and Vocational Training, Prof. Joyce Ndalichako, visited our BAME Programme. After hearing presentations from students about the BAME Programme and after surveying students' projects and their products, she declared that she was *speechless*. She was very pleased to learn that *experiential learning* is not only for science studies, but was also possible for business studies.

Currently, our programme is well networked with Team academy programmes around the world, including in UK, Finland, and US. We have been participating in the Socrates Sessions organized by the Tiimiakatemia Global, in Finland and also have been member of the Team Learning Community based in UK.

Since January, 2021, our BAME students have been working with students from Evergreen University in Washington State, USA, to establish cross-continent projects that will enhance their entrepreneurial learning while positively impacting the local community. So far, they have already established an international Non-Governmental Organization (NGO) whose common why reads as follows: *Together we create opportunities, build relationships through team entrepreneurship, connect US Changemakers with their global counterparts, and promote safeguard provisions in developing countries to empower equitable growth.* The NGO leadership is one based on co-leadership, i.e. every position is occupied by two students: one from US and another from Tanzania. So far, the students are in the process of starting and running two projects: a Recycling and 3D Printing project and a tomato and pepper processing project.

Conclusion

It is high time for a wider adoption of Team Academy Learning Philosophy in Tanzania in order to expedite this nation's prosperity. This chapter has shown how the University of Iringa implemented the BAME programme. Some lessons can be learned from the University of Iringa, which started these initiatives on its own rather than from external forces. One major lesson that has been learnt is that for an institution to break the inertia that has been built over many years depends on many factors that include: top management being fully supportive, faculty and staff being understanding and willing to change accordingly, availability of soft and hard infrastructure, availability of well trained and dedicated coaches, availability of resources to run the programme, and support from other actors in the entrepreneurship and innovation ecosystem.

References

AfDB, OECD, UNDP, UNECA. (2012). *African economic outlook 2012: Promoting youth employment.* African Development Bank, Organisation for Economic Co-operation and Development, United Nations Development Programme, United Nations Economic Commission for Africa. Paris: OECD publishing. https://youtheconomicopportunities.org/sites/default/files/uploads/resource/African%20Economic%20Outlook%202012.pdf

Bangu, N., Kuzilwa, J., Sabokwigina, D., & Mpogole, H. (2013). *Towards University— Industry linkage through entrepreneurial teaching and learning approaches in Tanzania: Experience from the University of Iringa.* Internal University of Iringa Report. Unpublished.

Chachage, B., Sabokwigina, D., Mpogole, H., Sessanga, Y., & Malima, G. (2021). Entrepreneurship in higher education institutions: The case of University of Iringa, Tanzania. In M. Lönnborg, O. B. Ndiege, & B. Tesfaye (Eds.), *Beyond borders: Essays on entrepreneurship, co-operatives and education in Sweden and Tanzania* (pp. 133–150). Huddinge: Södertörns högskola. www.diva-portal.org/smash/record. jsf?pid=diva2%3A1541493&dswid=-2965

Downey, M. (2003). *Effective coaching: Lessons from the coach's coach.* Cengage Learning. Knutsford: Texere publishing.

ILO. (2013). *Rethinking youth employment coordination in East Africa.* Dar es Salaam: International Labour Organization. www.ilo.org/wcmsp5/groups/public/ —africa/—ro-abidjan/—ilo-dar_es_salaam/documents/publication/wcms_ 241525.pdf

Isaacs, W. (1999). *Dialogue: The art of thinking together.* New York: Crown Business.

Katzenbach, J. R., & Smith, D. K. (2006). *The wisdom of teams: Creating the high-performance organization.* Boston, MA: Harvard Business School Press.

Kimelemeta, P. (2017, August 31). Watu 56,000 wagombea nafasi 400 TR. *Mtanzania.* https://mtanzania.co.tz/watu-56000-wagombea-nafasi-400-tra/

Marquart, M. J. (2004). *Optimizing the power of action learning: Solving problems and building leaders in real time.* .Palo Alto, CA: Davies-Black.

MHA. (2014, June 14). Watu zaidi ya 10000 waliojitokeza kwa usaili wa nafasi za kazi 70 Uhamiaji. *Mtangazaji.* www.mtangazaji.com/

Mwasalwiba, E., Dahles, H., & Wakkee, I. (2012). Graduate entrepreneurship in Tanzania: Contextual enablers and hindrances. *European Journal of Scientific Research, 76*(3), 386–402. https://core.ac.uk/download/pdf/143891618.pdf

Nonaka, I., & Takeuchi, H. (1995). *The knowledge-creating company: How Japanese companies create the dynamics of innovation.* Oxford: Oxford University Press.

Olomi, D. R., & Sabokwigina, D. (2010). Entrepreneurship education in Tanzanian Business Schools: A nationwide survey. In 12th International Conference on African Entrepreneurship and Small Business Development (ICAESB), Zanzibar, Tanzania, 6–7 May 2010.

Sabokwigina, D., & Mpogole, H. (2013). *Finnish Trip Report. Internal University of Iringa Report.* Unpublished.

Senge, P.M. (2006), *The Fifth Discipline: The Art and Practice of the Learning Organization,* Doubleday, New York, NY.

World Bank Group. (2014). *Tanzania: Productive jobs wanted.* Washington, DC: World Bank. http://documents1.worldbank.org/curated/en/539541468129886159/pdf/904340v10ESW0P0ec0Summary0ENG0final.pdf

9 The Story of TAZEBAEZ, the First Team Company of Mondragon Team Academy

Ainhoa Esnaola and Joanes Røsø

Introduction

TAZEBAEZ was seeded in the first-ever bachelor's degree in Entrepreneurial Leadership and Innovation (LEINN) of Mondragon Team Academy (MTA). This adventure started in 2009 in Irun, Basque Country, and after graduating, seven of the members of the original team company decided to continue their team entrepreneurial journey together. We established TAZEBAEZ as a cooperative firm in 2013, and since then, it has experienced many challenges, transformations, and adventures.

The biggest challenge was to find a business that would fit all of us that dared to dream and make the basic principle of cooperatives our mantra: as cooperativist one does not just contribute with work or capital, one must contribute with both work and capital for the common development of the cooperative and humanity.

2009–2013: #Team-Entrepreneurship #University

The essence and the spirit of the team company were born at that time, while we were studying LEINN. As we were the first-ever generation in MTA, we were not only team entrepreneurs, but also co-creators and co-founders of the MTA movement.

Since the very beginning innovation and uncertainty were present in our daily lives, which led us to name our team company TAZEBAEZ, that translates as *Why Not* in Basque. The name is connected to our roots and spirit and became our philosophy, as well as other representing sentences we embraced such as the one that the founder of Mondragon Business Group always use, *aurrera, beti aurrera* (Molina, 2005) which means *always moving ahead*.

The 4-years degree was an incredible learning platform. At the early ages of 18–22, we learnt to self-organize, leave behind a traditional learning

DOI: 10.4324/9781003163176-10

approach, and challenge ourselves every day. At certain times this process was challenging because our closest circle (family, friends, . . .) did not understand what we were doing, but this empowered us to build our own community. Throughout the 4 years we developed projects in the Basque Country, Spain, the Netherlands, and Brazil. Besides, and thanks to the learning journeys, we had the opportunity to further develop projects in Finland, USA, China, and India. These were developed together with the other team company of our generation, AKKUA, and others within and outside MTA and the Team Academy (TA) network. The projects were of different nature, but most of them focused on innovative education, communication, event management, cooperative development, international affairs, consultancy and projects with a social purpose linked to our values. TAZEBAEZ was also really involved in the expansion of the MTA model, working in different initiatives, such as the MTA Labs in Amsterdam, Bilbao, Madrid, and Valencia. We then began to understand two things above all: that the world goes beyond each one's home cities, and that people are more powerful and strong as a team.

By the end of our degree, 12 out of the 14 people who started LEINN graduated. During the 4 years of the programme, we were supported by many people all around the world, such as professionals from TA, the cooperative movement of Mondragon[1], and the Junior Enterprises[2] movement, but especially from our team coach, Jose Mari Luzarraga and the rest of the co-founders of LEINN at Mondragon University: Sari Veripa, Sain Lopez, and Aitor Lizartza.

2013–2016: #Cooperativism #Identity

On the day of the *24h birthgiving*,[3] one of the last challenges in LEINN, we decided to go to a notary and TAZEBAEZ was established as a cooperative. These spontaneous actions have been part of the essence of TAZE-BAEZ since we started, following one of the ideas we always embodied: *if it is not now, then when? And if it is not us, then who.* At that moment, we were not really sure how we would continue our journey after graduation, but we knew we would reach our goals by continuing to work hard and together.

We decided it would be interesting if many of us carried out the final dissertation projects in different key companies in some strategic areas of the Basque Country such as industry, strategic design, education, and international cooperation. This set a framework for our future way of working once the cooperative was formed.

During the first two years, 2013–2014, a few members were fully committed and most of the members had full-time jobs, but all of us were fully connected to the cooperative in heart and thought. We used to accept almost every opportunity from universities, governments, development agencies, MTA, and TA networks. We had members working in Bristol, Moscow, Jharkhand, Houston, Amsterdam, Madrid, Bilbao, and Valencia. The objective was to gain new knowledge, experience and have a stable monthly income.

This period that lasted almost 3 years may have been the most critical one. We realized that after finishing LEINN we did not have a clear business model, but we had the biggest and most precious assets that any company can have: the enthusiasm, energy, willingness, resilience and values to be a cooperative, and to make our dreams come true together.

In 2015, we realized that besides LEINNers, other profiles were also needed in the cooperative to become a more professional company. Not only did we need to define the profile of people we needed but this also involved interviewing and rejecting some very valid candidates. A finance manager and a graphic designer were the first two profiles we hired. After these, engineers, communication professionals, and educators have joined our project.

At the same time, some of the work we were doing around the world ended up being long-term projects, which ignited a reflection in the cooperative: was TAZEBAEZ an international multi-located company? Or was it simply offering services internationally? We realized that we had to define our value proposition in order to do business abroad because this would be key in our future strategy and development. This will also initiate an important debate in TAZEBAEZ, how did we go abroad? How did we remain connected with our fellow teammates abroad in order to support the projects and professional development as well as their personal wellbeing?

Figure 9.1 Happy New Year 2016 Video
Source: Tazebaez Team (2015)

Figure 9.2   Berdeago 2019 video
Source: Tazebaez Team (2019)

2016–2020: #Interdisciplinarity #Diversification

In 2016, we decided that it was time to join forces and grow by being closer than ever and by focusing on offering products as well as services. We decided that everyone had to be 100% focused on the business development of the company. Key people joined back to be full-time and based in the headquarters with specific challenges. My role was to lead, as full-time CEO, the new stage of growth and consolidation of the company.

We decided to set our focus on building high-performing teams and on creating sustainable businesses. One way of accelerating this process was to look for new synergies and initiatives. That is how we merged with another graduated team company from LEINN, which had two main brands: Make it Visual (MIV) and Berdeago.

MIV (Tazebaez S.Coop., 2020) offered graphic recording and communication services and Berdeago was the biggest sustainability fair organized annually in the Basque Country. Abilities were complementary, values were common and synergies were clear. The merger made TAZEBAEZ to face new challenges: how do we merge? What does TAZEBAEZ offer both to new and current members of the cooperative? We decided everyone needed to have the same rights and obligations. And in this process, we reaffirmed the idea that people trained in the MTA environment are able to function in high performing teams as a result of the training received and the culture generated during those 4 years.

Figure 9.3 New Branding Process video
Source: Tazebaez Team (2018)

TAZEBAEZ created a new mission statement at that time: *we are misfits, we transform people (always starting from ourselves and being aware that we are always 100% responsible for everything that happens around us) and we change the world* (Tazebaez S. Coop, 2016, n.d.). Thus, we focused on making an impact on already existing businesses and on creating new ones and we defined four expertise areas: education, business, product and service design, and communication.

Education – Travelling University

TAZEBAEZ designs team learning-based solutions for educational institutions and companies. After years of doing it, we wanted to start offering our own educational products. TAZEBAEZ launched *Travelling U*, our own *university* concept, in collaboration with MTA and Mondragon University, with the aim of exploring the MTA methodology from different angles. That is how we launched the 4-year bachelor's degree LEINN International in 2016, adding an international approach to the existing LEINN degree. LEINN International is a nomad degree (each course is carried out in a new country), participants come from all over the world (there is an average of 10 different nationalities per cohort), and a scholarship programme exists to support all of those candidates that despite having an amazing profile may have been left behind due to their personal economic situation. That is how the participants develop a high degree of multicultural empathy.

TAZEBAEZ-Travelling U was already a key agent in the MTA community, but then became a key strategic partner. This relationship opened plenty of opportunities in the expansion of our business to new markets and new institutional partnerships, especially in Asia, where we became the co-founders of MTA Labs in Shanghai and Seoul.

Figure 9.4   LEINN International Awake (Beyond COVID-19) video
Source: Leinn International (2020)

With Travelling U, we have worked on different educational organizations around the world, developing different programmes, such as Changemaker Lab, a program that develops entrepreneurial skills for regular university students in existing degrees, generating interdisciplinary projects, and team experiences. Changemaker Lab has become the first multidisciplinary and cross-faculty program ever implemented in many of these institutions.

Travelling U's so-called umbrella has become the home for new programmes that use the same methodology. Some of them have remained in collaboration with MTA such as TEAMINN, the renewed train-the-trainers programme to support the training of Team Coaches. Or LEINN Arts degree, our second international program, focused in Arts and cultural industries, launched in 2020 in collaboration also with Last Tour company. We also design and run all the international experiences for all the different LEINN degrees, a service that we have started selling to other universities.

Business – Innpulsory

TAZEBAEZ wanted their second expertise area to focus on offering solutions based on strategic design, entrepreneurship, and intrapreneurship with a human-centred design approach, in order to help organizations innovate and grow. These business services took the form of a consultancy company that we called *Innpulsory*. We have carried out projects with different entities at a national and international level, such as ULMA, Repsol, Ashoka, Unicef, Lantegi Batuak, Mondragon Group, Basque Government, and Osakidetza.

Innpulsory might have adopted different names depending on the projects, but it has been and it is one of the core businesses.

Product and Service Design – Innkubo

Going from offering services to products implied deep reflections and years of testing. One of the first products TAZEBAEZ launched was *The Makery*, a cooperative prototyping lab, for the design and creation of products, prototypes, and spaces, with the goal of democratizing the use of tech and interactive experiences to help educational institutions, companies, and individuals. Through The Makery, TAZEBAEZ gave birth to its first product, Polimaker, a thermoplastic material that becomes malleable when heated to 60 degrees, turning it into a plasticine-like product that could be used in the do-it-yourself world. A product that was not as successful as we thought it would be, but that helped us to learn.

The Makery gave TAZEBAEZ the opportunity to be close to different innovative organizations, which gave us the chance to learn and challenge ourselves to design our own methodology for launching product-based startups. This methodology was based on loops (Ries, 2011), and was designed to work both with agents outside and teampreneurs inside who wanted to launch new products. This is how a new expertise area inside the cooperative started, and we created then, the investment holding *Innkubo business* (our own venture builder) with one main objective: to generate new businesses in a new reality where different rules and players are established: start-ups, investments, and equity partners.

From Innkubo we are working on identifying key and disruptive emerging sectors (i.e. blockchain technology, the breeding of insects for human food, exponential education and sustainable mobility). Since Inkubo's creation in 2018, we became part of more than 11 companies and initiatives of different types, such as OX Motorcycles, InsektLabel Biotech, Meatze, etc.

Communication

Since the merger in 2016, Make it Visual (MIV) leads the process of using visual thinking to facilitate and improve communication and interaction between people, providing leadership, and clarity to the process both internally and as an external service offering comprehensive solutions for branding, web, motion graphics, illustration, signage, video, publisher or events. Design, communication and art have become part of our DNA.

Figure 9.5 Makeitvisual Website
Source: Makeitvisual (2019)

Key Learnings

It is difficult to make tangible how Team Academy methodology and the Mondragon Cooperative experience has impacted and shaped us, but we are aware that our transformation at a personal and team levels, as well as the understanding of the world and business in general, is highly influenced by both. Here are some of the key learnings from the experience lived over our 10 years of history as TAZEBAEZ:

Individual Servant Leadership: CEO = Chief Empathy Officer

Almost without realizing it, time goes by and you consider changing offices because the current one has no space anymore. When you go from sharing the project with 7 people to sharing it with 30, you realize people and leaders' responsibility has increased significantly, especially as a CEO.

As a cooperative, we put people at the centre of the project, and the main task of my role, the CEO, is to make everyone understand that they, are at the centre and the heart of the cooperative. A culture of self-responsibility is generated. Understanding this, at TAZEBAEZ we have joined the minority trend of changing the "*e*" of *executive* for the "*e*" of *empathy* in our CEO position. CEO stands for Chief Empathy Officer and their clear mission is to generate an empathic environment where people grow and develop.

Team Leadership: COOP Style for Internal Leadership #Kooperaktibistak

Tazebaez has experienced growth in terms of the number of people working in the cooperative and in the network. We've learnt that growth brings challenges in management and in the feeling of belonging. We also see how participation, democracy, ownership, self-management, voice, and vote are some of the values that people increasingly seek in their (work) life worldwide. We are closer than ever to the re-emergence of cooperatives as an exemplary movement.

However, we learnt with experience that in cooperatives and companies in which participation has been an intrinsic part of management, people lose awareness of commitment, accountability, self-responsibility and managerial reality. And when this happens, complaints arise, and it is difficult to re-generate a space of trust in which people have a proactive, constructive, and positive attitude that fosters a passion for work and personal development.

Thus, the commitment to re-inspire comes from the need to return to the roots of democratic and participatory processes, to reconnect with the core values of the cooperative. In order to re-generate the identity, social commitment, and the flame of belonging of our members, we create internal spaces for mirroring, debating, and dialoguing, such as project and team meetings, team days, summer and winter camps or member assemblies. We use specially designed visual tools and dynamics to support our own methodology and style. The key relies on turning these dynamics into CULTURE, reinforcing the recognition of proactivity and participation.

Ekintzaile: Activist + Entrepreneur in a Team of Teams for Humanity

We believe collective sovereignty needs to be reinforced for a positive global change, and that *teampreneurship* is one of the tools to promote these new economic models. The word *ekintzaile* in Basque is composed of two English words *entrepreneur* and *activist*, and that is our understanding of what teampreneurs must do: to immerse themselves in providing solutions.

It is true that the word entrepreneur is often associated with individual success, but we are believers of the power of being entrepreneurs in teams. Yes, it can be harder to operate collectively sometimes and it can also take us out of our comfort zone; but not only goals are achieved faster together, but the team and the collective will also go further, and at a much higher level of stability.

Entrepreneurship cannot be the only answer to the global crisis. A crisis refers to a situation in which a person, organization, or society does not correspond to its proper or normal functioning. These situations demand change and adaptation, yet in some cases where the structure of the system is shaken, may lead to a revolution. This is our proposal in order to mutate perception and to hack the system: to swallow the red pill that Morpheus gives Neo in Matrix (Wachowski & Wachowski, 1999); the path towards awareness and social responsibility.

In order to gradually transform society, the system must be affected from as many places as possible. The nonconformists, those of us who hack the system, make a call for you to be conscious, organize and join the revolution. The revolution of collective sovereignty, to build alternatives and to apply new schemes. Because happiness is only complete when it is shared. As Che Guevara said, *If there is no organisation, ideas lose their effectiveness after the first impulse* (Archivo Juventudes, n.d., p. 3). We need to bring out the revolution, the spark that we carry within and organize ourselves, in a distributed, digital, global, and local way.

2020 and Beyond: #Renewal

At different times in life, taking distance is relative. When you are a child, going from your home to the town square seems like going far away, as you grow up the sense of distance changes, and *going away* means going on a journey far away from home, from your town or even from your country. It is undeniable that for the people who make TAZE-BAEZ, the journey is not only a way of experimenting, learning, and growing, but a search for fulfilment, a way to find happiness and wisdom. We connect with Aristotle's statement *happiness is the meaning and the purpose of life, the whole aim and end of human existence* (Gilbert, 2010, p. 533). We know each person has their own and evolving meaning of happiness, passion, mission, ambitions, and set of talents. We want to be the platform where each one of us can let all the others to flourish, for good.

How can you project yourself for the future? The Ikigai theory (García & Miralles (2017) helps us define our ideal project-employment on an individual level. But this gets complicated when, in addition to the 30–40 people who make up your team, you must scale this concept to the community. This is one of the greatest challenges for 21st-century organizations, as well as for TAZEBAEZ: to find a balance between personal and professional aspirations.

So, let's travel back in time to gain perspective. We go back to the origin of the Mondragon cooperative movement, with the gaze of the youth of the 1950s, but with the vision behind the lenses of Don José María

Arizmendiarrieta, the founder of Mondragon Corporation, a person who knew how to bring together work, dignity, meaning, and ambition of people who, a priori, were destined to darkness. Human nature tends to envision past times as better, perhaps because of the fear of facing new realities. But it isn't, it only perpetuates the message: don't *try, don't push yourself.*

However, every rule has its exception, and that is us. The committed and creative alternative of young people working in cooperation (cooperativists), of those who (actively) decide to reinvent everything, those who swim against the status quo, the (dis)comfort, fighting for a fairer and more equitable society, more sustainable at environmental, human and economic levels. A better society, a better world. Arizmendiarrieta constantly shows us a light in the shadow, an inspiration of a community united in cooperation, capable of creating a referent business group; also, making the Basque Country as one of the most egalitarian regions with the best quality of life, serving as an inspiration to the world, acting with responsibility and courage. As the Chinese proverb Arizmendiarrieta used to repeat *it is better to light up a match than to curse darkness* (Azurmendi, 1984, p. 211). Calling for action, instigating minds to reflect and voices to raise, not to just remind us of the values of cooperation but to understand and generate the new philosophy of cooperatives. Strong, proud, just, OURS.

We come closer to the end of our temporal journey by coming back to the present, saying that we know it, we appreciate it, and we believe in it. We want to contribute to the dissemination of this alternative way of life. To be the people that make cooperation their life project.

We need to connect with both local and global initiatives, generations and cultures, to inspire action and show that another way of doing business and transforming the world is possible. Therefore, in addition to being part of the local cooperative initiatives, in 2015, we co-founded and served the board of the Young European Cooperators' Network (YECN) and one of our colleagues is the representative VP for Europe at the International Cooperative Alliance youth executive committee (ICA Youth Network). As TAZEBAEZ we have also continued learning and improving our way of working, getting inspired by different models, such as The Connected Company (Gray & Wal, 2012).

Currently, we are working on the (r)evolution of cooperative governance aiming for its worldwide expansion digitally. We are part of the development of the DisCO project (DisCo, n.d.), (Distributed Cooperative Organization) an economic P2P Commons, cooperative and feminist alternative to Decentralized Autonomous Organizations (DAOs).

In short, DisCO makes people work together cooperatively, grounded and focused on the common good in a digital way. This type of governance was initially extracted from a collective called Guerrilla Translation, and currently, from DisCO. Moreover, as we are the first case study of MTA World and we sincerely believe that the digital cooperative movement is the mainstream model of economic development for good in the 21st century, we are applying what we have learned in TAZEBAEZ over these years. We are taking action once again, thinking slowly but acting incessantly.

If you want to learn more about DisCO, download the manifesto and the elements, and join the party. Shall we dance? Don't let the music stop.

Notes

1 The Mondragon Corporation is a corporation and federation of worker cooperatives based in the Basque region of Spain. It is the largest cooperative group in the world. It was founded in the town of Mondragon in 1956 by José María Arizmendiarrieta and a group of his students at a technical college he founded.
2 Junior Enterprises (JEs) are non-profit companies run entirely by university students. They provide services, in their fields of study, to other companies, entrepreneurs and society as a whole.
3 A Team Academy (TA) tool that can be named differently in the different initiatives of the TA network, but that consists in being a team process, where everyone takes part and new knowledge or solution is created.

References

Archivo Juventudes. (n.d.). Ernesto Che Guevara: Qué debe ser un joven comunista. *La caja de herramientas Biblioteca virtual UJCE* [online]. http://archivo.juventudes.org/textos/Ernesto%20Che%20Guevara/Que%20debe%20ser%20un%20joven%20comunista.pdf

Azurmendi, J. (1984). *El hombre cooperativo: pensamiento de Arizmendiarrieta*. Mondragon: Caja Laboral Popular, Lan Kide Aurrezkia..

García, H., & Miralles, F. (2017). *Ikigai: the Japanese secret to a long and happy life*. London: Hutchinson

DisCO— (n.d.). Distributed Cooperative Organizations. *DisCO.Coop*. https://disco.coop/.

Gilbert, P. (2010). Seeking inspiration: The rediscovery of the spiritual dimension in health and social care in England. *Mental Health, Religion & Culture, 13*(6), 533–546.

Gray, D., & Wal, T. V. (2012). *The connected company* (1st ed.). Sebastopol, CA: O'Reilly Media.

Makeitvisual. (2019). *Nosotras*. https://makeitvisual.es/nosotras/

Molina, F. (2005). *José María Arizmendiarrieta 1915–1976. Biografía*. Mondragon: Caja Laboral-Euskadiko Kutxa.

LeinnInternational.(2020,March31).Awake(Beyondcovid-19).#TravellingUniversity. *YouTube*. www.youtube.com/watch?v=z0CBgUTZEcg

Ries, E. (2011). *The lean startup*. New York: Crown Publishing.

Tazebaez S. Coop. (2016). *Hola*. https://tzbz.coop/es/language/

Tazebaez S. Coop. (2020, March 31). *Visual thinking*. https://makeitvisual.es/

Tazebaez S. Coop. (n.d.). *LEINN international*. https://leinninternational.com/

Tazebaez Team. (2015, December 30). #UrteBerri_ON_2016. *Vimeo* [video]. https://vimeo.com/150370054

Tazebaez Team. (2018, May 7) New branding process | TAZEBAEZ. *Vimeo* [video]. https://vimeo.com/268356286

Tazebaez Team. (2019, February 13). Berdeago Azoka 2019. *Vimeo* [video]. https://vimeo.com/317002195

Wachowski, A., & Wachowski, L. (1999). *The matrix*. [Motion picture]. United States: Warner Bros. Pictures.

10 Team Academy Pioneers in the UK

A Team Entrepreneurs' Perspective

Beth Williams

Introduction

In this chapter I will be sharing an insight into my personal experience of being a part of the first Team Academy programme in the UK (2013–2016). Myself and my fellow Team Entrepreneurs were, we believe, trailblazers, as we had to find the solution to not only establishing a new/start up business individually and collectively but also simultaneously translating associated criteria into an academically accredited degree. This chapter will be an emotive personal reflection about my experience whilst undertaking the degree; I will be reflecting on some external perceptions experienced on the degree and what impact that had on myself and my fellow Team Entrepreneurs. I will be exploring where I am now and what I have experienced since graduating from the degree. I will also include a reflection on how I feel, 4 years later, and what impact the Team Entrepreneurship (TE) degree has had on my personal life as well as my career journey. Throughout this chapter I will be touching on and quoting directly from some of my fellow first UK cohort team members, as this will provide a contrasting insight into their experience. All conversations took place during 2020; initially an informal discussion took place over email but to solidify the data a formal questionnaire was completed by each team member.

The Drivers to Join TE

Prior to attending the University of the West of England open day, my educational background was very traditional, it was at the open day that I stumbled across the TE degree and a new style of "learning by doing" through entrepreneurial activities. Instantly intrigued, I enquired about how the degree would be structured and when I discovered the main premise of the degree was for individuals and teams to create and build their own business, it seemed like a perfect fit. I have always had an entrepreneurial mindset

DOI: 10.4324/9781003163176-11

and my aim has always been to start my own business and with the TE degree I was able to do this whilst undertaking the academic rigour required to complete a traditional degree. I stumbled across the degree whilst meeting with traditional business degree lecturers; after meeting with Dr. Carol Jarvis I gained a more, in depth understanding of TE and how Team Entrepreneurs could build businesses whilst personally developing and building theoretical knowledge around business as a whole.

My preferred learning style is through doing and or visual, and I previously found exam-based assessments to be difficult and not an accurate reflection of my capabilities. I have always flourished in team-based activities and independent learning and creative learning tasks. The concept of connecting like-minded individuals with similar goals and visions was an exciting prospect and this was something I had not previously experienced. On reflection, at the time I wasn't 100% sure as to what the degree would look like or how it would work but I was eager to give it a go, and I think this forms part of a vital mindset of anyone wanting to complete a TE degree. We were aware from the beginning that this degree was a trial, the course leaders needed to prove the degree's validation and it was certainly out of the comfort zone for a traditional academic institution.

One of the main aspects of the TE degree is predominantly team work. We were encouraged to create teams which could perform highly through undertaking business activities as well as reflecting on theoretical knowledge and processes which we could share with each other. Teamwork and collaborative learning is at the centre of this degree and it was one of the key factors that attracted me. It seemed daunting to create a business by myself but the idea of being able to build a business with a team of individuals who have a different set of skills but with the same vision was exciting. The Team Academy model actually fosters risk taking and provides a safe place to create and develop entrepreneurial activity.

There were 2 team companies in the first cohort, each team consisting of around 20 individuals; there were only 5 females in total across the cohort. Lucy Long was a fellow first cohort TE, from my own team company who actually left the degree in the first year, she moved to a traditional Business Management degree; it's interesting to gauge her personal view of why she was originally attracted to TE. Lucy explains *The prominent factors that stood out for me were the fact that the learning would be more practical, simulating real life experiences with a business. It appeared that a lot of team work and collaboration would be involved, which I much preferred than working individually. It seemed a very unique way of learning* (personal communication, 6 September 2020). Lucy chose to leave the TE programme shortly after joining as she required a more traditional method of learning, she preferred a lecture style method as this was a more tangible form of gaining the overall business management knowledge she required. The TE degree is quite a self-managed process, which requires TEs to learn what is required as and when they need it, based on the development stage of their business. As there were no formal traditional "lecturers" that provided direct theories and practices, the methodology did not suit some individuals' learning requirements.

Jasmine Sommers was also fellow first cohort team entrepreneur who was in a different team company to myself. When asked what attracted Jasmine to the degree, her response was as follows; *I was originally planning to study a conventional business degree at University. I was unsure what to do but wanted to pick something that was broad enough I could take anywhere with me after I left university. When I was told about the Team Entrepreneurship degree I was really interested; mainly because the course was practical and was based on actual learning rather than theory* (personal communication, 17 September 2020). Jasmine had a very similar experience like me at the open day. It's important to explain that the Team entrepreneurship degree was not actively being marketed during the open day so there was very little and vague brief descriptions of it, it was only after actively enquiring about the degree that we both discovered more about it.

Discovering the Team Academy programme was at the time, what seemed a "by chance" encounter, as the recruitment and marketing for the programme was certainly not as prominent in comparison to other degree programmes. It was not the knowledge that this degree would be *the first of its kind in the UK.* that attracted me to the programme instead, it was more about the learning styles that were implemented and the team-based challenges. Myself and my fellow team entrepreneurs were clearly attracted to the independent style of learning and building businesses whilst completing a traditional degree.

Being "first of its kind" was not the deciding factor however, as team entrepreneurs, we felt we were certainly trailblazers; we were penguins but, for me and for many more of my colleagues we were excited by this concept, the fact we were able to help build and create something that would encourage innovation, leaders and entrepreneurship.

I also asked Jasmine Sommers what she knew about the programme prior to joining, *I knew quite a lot about the course as I had done quite a bit of research. I knew I would be the first year in the U.K to attend this course but had read that it had been tried and tested in Finland and had proven to be very successful. I was particularly keen because the course did not include exams and had a lot of practical based learning* (personal communication, 17 September 2020). I am sure many of the first U.K cohort Team Entrepreneurs read up about the Finnish model and its proven success but it was interesting to experience how this model would be adapted into the UK.

There was certainly a transition period from leaving a traditional educational format and experience to then coming into this new style of learning. For some individuals it was a very easy and comfortable transition but for others it was of course much more difficult. One of the reasons I believe I found the transition into the "learning by doing" methodologies a positive one, is that I personally had struggled with fitting into the more rigid, perhaps more traditional educational structures we have here in the UK. I believe this certainly has had an impact on where myself and my fellow Team Entrepreneurs are now, what we are currently undertaking and what we took away from the programme.

It's About the Attitude and Process

I believe it's important for all Team Entrepreneurs to have a particular set of behaviours and skills in order to succeed on this programme, it is a mindset that requires determination, self-reflection, self-motivation, inquisitiveness, hardworking, and team work; these are all essential in adopting the TE methods. It is difficult to explain the TE programme instead, it requires full immersion before you can truly understand it.

Fowle and Jussila (2016, p. 4) highlight an interesting view on how a new Team Entrepreneur can interpret the programme, their article quotes *as the programme developed, we observed student responses to the innovative combination of freedom and responsibility. We needed a way to encourage the more useful behaviours and discourage the ones that were a barrier to effective learning* (Clouder et al., 2013, p. 4).

In many ways the programme leaders and coaches were "learning by doing" alongside us, of course they had the key components of the structures and assessments, but I imagine it was incredibly difficult for them to understand how a Finnish educational model would translate into the U.K educational system.

For me, something clicked when I first joined the cohort I instantly knew that this educational and personal experience was a perfect fit for me. I understood the value of independent and reflective learning, the "learning by doing" concept just made sense. It felt like a Silicon Valley start-up; days packed with enthusiasm and new ideas.

My initial impressions were that there wasn't much structure which I very quickly realized was a huge positive to the course. For some, of course, this proved to be quite difficult, especially after coming from and being comfortable in an educational background which was very much traditional in its style of teaching. Some of the Team Entrepreneurs struggled with the lack of structure and scarcity of traditional "teaching" which of course is not an aspect of the Team Academy methodologies. No exam-based assessments was also something that attracted a lot of individuals to the programme; after joining the programme and receiving the academic assessment requirements, a number of Team Entrepreneurs came to the realization that just because there would be no exams this does not mean the academic assessments would be "easier" than a traditional degree programme.

However, the academic assessments required on a Team Academy programme are much more rigorous, timely and detailed with, every single assessment being considered, thought out and beneficial in the journey of building a business. It was soon after joining the programme that the vast amount of challenging academic assessments became clear and this discouraged some Team Entrepreneurs. For me though, I was enjoying reflective assessments, so it seemed a perfect fit for me.

It was made very clear by the programme leaders that this way of learning would not suit all individuals; everyone learns in different ways; some are more visual while others are more traditional and prefer to be taught and to have that structure. The way I always tried to explain the degree to people was that we were all attempting to create and grow a real-life business whilst completing a business degree at the same time which of course includes all of the academic assessments.

Trailblazers: Comfort, Discomfort, and Readiness

In three words I would say my first impression of the programme would be *comfort, discomfort,* and *readiness.* I felt at ease and comfortable because for the first time in my education I understood and saw the value of these learning methods, I felt uncomfortable because I was pushing myself out of my comfort zone in trailing something I had always wanted to achieve, creating my own business and I had to complete this alongside a group of people at that point, I knew nothing about. Lastly, I felt ready, ready to start and jump straight into this challenging new chapter of my personal and academic development.

We felt we were indeed "trailblazers", being the first degree of its type in the UK meant we had a lot of proving to do, not only to the university itself but to our course leaders, wider communities and ourselves.

Prior to, and during, the programme we were aware that aspects of the structure and assessment criteria would change and develop as the course went on. As a cohort split into two teams we were told we would receive seed capital of around £5,000 from the university and then it would be down to the individual teams to decide how that fund would be distributed amongst the individual projects. However, after enrolling in the programme, a few months in, we were made aware that we would, in fact, not be receiving this seed capital. Whilst this was a shock to each team I felt as though this was a good opportunity for us as budding entrepreneurs. It's a great life lesson to have; when it comes to setting up and creating your own business you aren't just handed investment with no criteria to meet. I believe this was a great opportunity for the teams to come together and invest their own funding or to find and apply for external funding. Of course, this is all part of the "real life experience" we were all there to have. Our understanding being, that given the unique nature of this programme, there were challenges around administration and delivery being experienced by the University, unlike our counterparts in Finland.

The programme was still in its early developmental stage. There were therefore and understandably, many blurry lines as to what we were and weren't able to do. Whilst we were encouraged to undertake whichever entrepreneurial activity we chose, there were also some boundaries as to what we could and couldn't do due to the fact we were still part of the academic institution. There was a back and forth questioning as to whether the university could have a say in what projects we were able to pursue; if the university was liable or not, etc. However, with the unknown came great opportunity, as we were able to trial and test different concepts with the backing and resources of a large educational organization and with the accreditation that comes with that.

Perceptions About the Programme

I took a huge amount of pride in explaining to people I met that I was part of this new learning methodology, and I was able to build and grow my own business whilst completing a business degree qualification, and I am still to this day. I created and built The Learning Expedition Company; we delivered learning expeditions to Businesses and Academic Institutions with the aim of using the Team Academy methodologies to solve the problems they were facing. Though this company was concluded by myself after graduating from the programme, it has still continued to develop and grow as a concept across other UK. Team Academy programmes to this day.

In most cases it was certainly a fantastic conversation topic and within the university and business community there was a great deal of interest, admiration, and excitement around the programme. Specifically, within the university, it was seen very positively.

Frequently we would be invited to attend networking events where we would be asked to provide talks about the degree and the specific business ventures we were undertaking. There was also the opportunity for potential collaboration with other departments within the university, for example, there was collaboration between the robotic department and a project group within my team. But, of course, with the positive does come some negative; there were academic individuals within the university who struggled to comprehend this style of learning, which is so far away from the traditional style they are used to. There were some negative comments around the lack of exams and how we were assessed in order to achieve our degree. Still to this day, when someone asks me about my degree qualification, there is always a response of pure excitement and interest.

Broadly, the perception from business owners and the wider community was fantastic and it certainly caused a "buzz". A significant range of opportunities became available to us and there was also some exciting media coverage. Jamie Rawsthorne, a fellow first year cohort in my team company explains that *I capitalised on it being a new and innovating degree. . . . I think in general people were curious and university staff were eager to make it work* (personal communication, 6 September 2020). Lucy Long stated *The majority of individuals I spoke to where intrigued about the course and it's approach* (personal communication, 10 September 2020); while Jasmine Sommers explained that *everyone I spoke to was extremely positive about the course. It was really exciting to explain how different it is to people and local businesses really took an interest into the concept. It was particularly good to see how much support we got from businesses as well, they were always keen to get involved in projects and offer services where they could* (personal communication, 17 September 2020).

The Journey Continues

Four years on and I am reflecting on my journey following graduation from the programme. Any transition period from University to employment is a difficult one for many. Indeed for me, leaving the Team Academy programme and moving into employment was certainly challenging. I had set up a company during my three years on the programme which I successfully ran. However, I made the decision to move away from this business and chose to seek employment opportunities upon leaving University. I had not only developed personally during the programme, but my knowledge of running a business as a whole was vastly improved; the learning I took from the programme in respect to how to set up and run my own business was invaluable. My decision to take up paid employment on graduation was in no way a reflection on the course, but rather a factual position in life I found myself at. I needed to go away, experience further working life beyond University life and earn some money to allow me to live and save for future business ventures.

Whilst being part of the degree course provided me with a safe place to test, learn, and fail, it was also a programme that forced me to try something that I had always wanted to achieve, setting up of my own company.

It's safe to say that over the 3 years on the programme my team company became a high performing team, of course, we still had much improvement to make, but on reflection to where I am now, the Team Academy team company I was part of has been the highest performing team I have ever worked in.

That in itself has been a challenge since graduating, the culture of teams. A team company encourages open communication, reflection, and difficult conversations in constructive and affective ways, whereas, my experience of working in teams since the programme has been quite the opposite and this really has been a challenge.

During those moments, the interactions we were having as a team company were vital and critical to the team's development as well as my own personal development. Once you have experienced a high performing team it is then quite difficult to be a part of another team that lacks this, now of course high performing teams are built on the cornerstone of a good culture, but within "open employment", sadly a lot of the teams I became a part of were already formed and their cultures were quite the opposite.

Following graduation, I moved into a role within a small tech start up based in Bristol, I then moved into a role within an international travel company. Myself and my partner then chose to travel around the world, this was a really significant experiential and reflective opportunity, and one which had a significant impact on me and in shaping how I moved forward in my life.

I reflected on my experience during the programme and how much I enjoyed being part of a team and running my own business. Upon returning to the UK I reconnected with some of my fellow team entrepreneurs, coaches and contacts, after reconnecting with Alison Fletcher (UK Team Academy promoter) I was offered the opportunity to take part in Team Mastery. Team Mastery provided me with another opportunity to be part of a team. It was also an incredibly powerful reflective journey for myself and the team; it was exciting and stimulating to be a part of the Team Academy community once again.

As I mentioned earlier, my travelling around the world enabled me to stop and reflect; I knew my aim would be to set up another company on our return, so this was a great opportunity for me to brainstorm new concepts. Indeed, it was in Cambodia where I came up with my current business idea. I was astonished and equally distressed by the amount of plastic on the beaches and in the seas, and the fact that a high volume of this were UK brands, our rubbish was ending up in their seas!

Upon returning to the UK I researched into the single use plastic consumption focusing on our bathrooms, it was then I identified an opportunity to not only do some good, but one that also provided me a platform to develop and establish a new business model. I wanted to build a business which would sell plastic free alternatives to haircare, skincare, and home fragrance items. I have built an online marketplace business model called

OKO Marketplace, where you can find natural, plastic-free, and vegan-friendly alternatives to the everyday personal care items, some of which are made by myself and others come from small, UK makers.

My previous experience during Team Academy was hugely beneficial to the creation of OKO Marketplace and I also utilized my network of Team Entrepreneurs in many ways. Prior to the Team Academy programme, I would have lacked the confidence to build a business with others let alone to build a business by myself.

It's fascinating to see where my fellow Team Entrepreneurs are now, and what they have achieved as well. Some of them have continued to grow their businesses which they set up during the programme, others have moved into employment and some have created and built new businesses. Jamie Rawsthorne, a fellow Team Entrepreneur spent the programme growing and developing an analytics company, however he is now running a six figure YouTube channel, advising on a Record Label and also selling an Amazon product. Lucy Long is currently working as an account manager for eBay classified groups, and has been doing so for two years. Her plan is to run her own business, but she firstly would like to gain as much learning and commercial experience as possible. Finally, Jasmine Sommers is employed by a small house builder based in Bath, she manages a building site of around 50 employees.

Re-connecting with my fellow Team Entrepreneurs highlighted that the team companies did not continue; following graduation it seems that we all very much went on our own paths. The conversations gathered may show individual career paths away from a team company however, the sense of community, resources and connection to Team Academy and the team companies is still very much present.

I fully believe that The Team Academy programme and learning methodologies have given me the knowledge, skills, and confidence to create and build my own business, but equally it has also provided me with the skills which make me a well-rounded and desirable employee. There are many opportunities that arise from this programme and the Team Academy network, I have met some like-minded individuals who have helped shape me into the person I am today, and I can say that the programme put me on a path of happiness and success.

References

Clouder, L., Broughan, C., Jewell, S., & Steventon, G. (Eds.). (2013). *Improving student engagement and development through assessment: Theory and practice in higher education.* Abingdon: Routledge.

Fowle, M., & Jussila, N. (2016). The adoption of a Finnish Learning Model in the UK. In *11th European Conference on Innovation and Entrepreneurship,* Newcastle.

Concluding Thoughts

Contributors' Conversation

Berrbizne Urzelai and Elinor Vettraino

Throughout this fourth book of the *Routledge Focus on Team Academy* series you will have met a number of researchers, practitioners, and learners all working with the Team Academy model and philosophy of entrepreneurial team learning. What follows is an amalgamation of a number of conversations that have taken place over the development of the *Team Academy in Diverse Settings* book, along with responses to some core questions about the place and the context in which Team Academy has been implemented. To help focus the thinking about the model, we invited authors to consider responses to questions around what from Team Academy attracted them, what they have learnt throughout their TA journey, and where they think TA should go next. The emerging conversations that follow offer some indication of some of the contributors' thoughts about the model and approach.

BERRBIZNE URZELAI: Given we are all on the same boat, I would like to know . . . what from Team Academy hooked you in? Ainhoa, you, for instance, have been one of the first team entrepreneurs graduated in MTA so what attracted you back then?

AINHOA ESNAOLA: Well, it was based on experiences more than in content, it gave us the opportunity to create deep relationships with our teammates and the community, to experiment different fields and discover ourselves, and to explore different cultures through travelling to places for an extended period of time. In sum, it was an opportunity to enjoy, challenge ourselves, and train for life!

BETH WILLIAMS: I resonate with some of that Ainhoa. For me as one of the first TA graduates in the UK, TA provided the opportunity to learn by doing whilst setting up a business. The concept of practically learning and reflecting was much more attractive to me than a traditional degree programme. I had always wanted to set up my own business and I knew from an early age that running my own business was a journey I wanted

DOI: 10.4324/9781003163176-12

to undertake so the concept of being able to complete a degree whilst setting up my own venture was ideal. TA also encouraged me to actually come to university, as prior to finding out about that programme I did not have the desire to attend university. *Self-discovered learning* makes so much sense to me and before learning about TA I had never known that the *learning by doing* concept existed.

ELINOR VETTRAINO: And what about others? We not only have team coaches in the room but also other entrepreneurship education practitioners and educators, academics, and people working around innovation. I would like to know your views.

DUNCAN IRACI: I was interested in the approach due to the hands-on nature of the learning, this is something that always made sense to me and it is my preferred way of really understanding, at a deeper level, how something really works, therefore, TA methodologies always made perfect sense to me.

DEO SABOKWIGINA: Yes, the experiential learning approach resonated well with me too. Indeed, the Tanzania education culture has been theory/academic-oriented and this has resulted in lots of jobless graduates in the country. These graduates lack job skills demanded by employers. They also lack business skills to start and grow a successful business. They also have a negative mindset towards starting and running a business. After learning about the TA learning philosophy, I knew that adopting this approach would help us produce enterprising graduates that are ready to face the challenges of the real-world after graduation.

PÄIVI RIMPILÄINEN: In our projects we have been looking for solutions for adults on-the-job learning. Team learning was found for this purpose. Then we started our co-operation with Team Academy Global.

NATALIA CERUTI: exactly. It is not only about university students. I was absolutely charmed by the place where the learning process was put, the importance and time that was given to it, going an extra mile from just learning outcomes. I saw happy, committed learners, struggling to improve their skills and still being accountable for their actions.

HAJIME IMAMURA: yes, for us TA fits our idea of *team play* in Japan. And also the profit-achieving target for all students in the real undergraduate university, that can't be conceivable in the Japanese university education. And mostly, I was really fascinated by the educational contents and methodology TA imported from Finland and modified by MTA itself. This is a really creative and innovative entrepreneurship education model.

WENDY WU: I am sure Hajime you are familiar with Taoism and you know what, TA is fundamentally rooted in experiential learning and has aspects which remind me of Chinese Taoism! I have to say that TA has transformed me personally so I'd like to influence more entrepreneurs, future thinkers and change makers to use it to help improve society.

GEORGIANA ELS: let me stay with you both in Asia for a while as I was actually hooked during a walking workshop on the paths of the Himalayas. It was sold to me by the people who were part of the movement. I think TA is made of people and its global community and what that represents should be cherished and continued.

BERRBIZNE: How interesting. It is clear that the experiential learning ingredient of TA was one of the secrets of the magic potion for many of you, but also the human community dimension of the movement.

ROBERTA SOGAYAR: yes, and the possibility to look at the future, the possibility to do what was right to do in education. I was looking for real and qualitative innovation and when I learned about it I could envision all the theories of education I had been studying combined in one specific approach.

TOMAS SPARANO: yes, and obviously the bonding experience created by team learning too. The feeling that we could do anything by trusting each other and exploring new ventures together to solve problems and deliver incredible experiences to team members and the stakeholders directly and indirectly involved in our projects.

GEORGINA DANCE: exactly Tomas. When I met and observed some teampreneurs for the first time I saw the most authentic relationship I had ever seen between learners in a degree setting. They were really invested in each other and genuinely worked together as a unit. I witnessed the power of the team and how it could be harnessed.

ELINOR: so, given that you have applied TA in very different settings and some of you that have been teampreneurs in TA programmes, can I ask you how has the TA approach helped you in your career?

GEORGIANA: I would say TA is a career in itself! TA has changed my approach to learning and doing and hence, changed the ways in which I view and plan my career. After graduation of the TA Mastery course, I have been able to implement the methods in teaching, research, and community projects and thus, I have been able to progress in my profession.

JOANES ROSO: Spot on Georgiana. During our university degree, we already started designing our lives and our careers, so in a way we made TA style our *way of living*. You learn how to learn and unlearn faster and better. You polish your curiosity, training yourself to make questions, digesting responses, and creating proposals.

DUNCAN: yes because TA encourages you to learn new things, to work with a wide variety of people and to adopt and try out new ways of working, communicating and viewing the business and educational world.

TOMAS: For me TA has helped me in many ways, but mainly to engage in projects that I could never have dreamed of before. The TA approach helped me develop self-confidence, creativity, leadership and social awareness.

BERRBIZNE: it definitely adds a much more dynamic varnish to the way we learn and work and gives us a *meaning*.

NATALIA: absolutely. TA approached helped me understand that I am a fan of the learning process, and hence that became my WHY.

GEORGINA: yes and it gave my pedagogy a home! Through my engagement with TA I have been able to be part of creating something at UWE I am truly proud of. It has given my work more meaning and reward.

TUULA KOIVUKANGAS: that is why our own teaching has changed towards coaching and this has expanded job opportunities. Team learning has also taught the courage to engage in dialogue.

WENDY: Yes, the insights and experiences I gained through TA has helped me to develop myself and improve my coaching too. TA ideas have infused everything I do and it has provided me the foundation to dare to be who I am.

DEO: definitely Wendy. I would also say it has helped me to develop myself and improve my coaching skills. I have been able to inspire and influence many students to become entrepreneurs and this makes me feel proud really. Since we introduced the TA learning programme at our University, we have been receiving many visitors from Embassies, Ministries, Agencies and other Universities who come to learn what we are doing in the TA programme. All visitors are wowed by what they see and this makes me feel that I have been making a contribution to the society's well-being.

HAJIME: for me as a university professor, TA helped me to motivate students in the active learning environment. As Deo says, this is a huge driver. Especially, to promote Entrepreneurship mindset among students, learning journey to MTA in Spain, especially in Bilbao is an excellent opportunity to inspire students. From several feedbacks from the students, I can see that the educational outcome is really enormous.

ROBERTA: And I would not say it is just about entrepreneurship. For me personally TA gave me so many insights about life in general, people, much less on entrepreneurship, and more on *peopleship*. It made me dig deeper about the things I wanted and I could become an entrepreneur of my higher self. It's hard to say about money . . . but I am a much more successful person in life in general due to what TA has brought to me.

BERRBIZNE: "peopleship", I love it. It definitely encompasses those two dimensions of people and business.

BETH: Certainly it does. I have always known creating and running my own business was something I had wanted to achieve and TA certainly accelerated that goal for me. It gave me the confidence, skills, and knowledge to take the jump in starting my own business but it also taught me that a typical 9–5 job would not suit me at all. TA showed me how to manifest and nurture my skills and knowledge and to utilize them not only in a business but also in my professional and personal development. TA moulded me into a business leader but it also taught me how to be a great employee by understanding what I would want to look for in an employer myself.

BERRBIZNE: And that is so important, right? To understand not only what you want to do and where you want to do but also the paths that you do not want to take. Now, as the title of this book is *TA in diverse settings*, I would not like to end this conversation without asking you where (which setting) you think TA should go next.

GEORGIANA: Adaptation and flexibility are key! From an academic perspective I see the TA model expanding outside of the core format, taking various shapes – postgraduate studies, other areas of study, various levels – from primary to masters. However, it would be important to preserve its philosophy and leading principles.

WENDY: TA should go to the mainstream, and global. It can benefit people in all areas of their life.

DUNCAN: Yes there could be a wide range of next steps, or settings for the TA model, one that makes perfect sense to me would be the application of the methodology in schools and sixth form colleges, to try to install an extra layer of critical thinking and wider perspective of the business world. At the same time, numerous TA methodologies could benefit many organizations, businesses, and teams in general, in terms of productivity, engagement, and stakeholdership of our modern working environments.

ELINOR: yes and in Finland that has been developed much more than in the UK so there is a lot still to do. Päivi and Tuula know a lot about this.

PÄIVI: We think team learning should be Civic Skill. In a complex world we need dialogue skills. All children and young people should have the opportunity to practice team learning skills in schools.

HAJIME: I hope it will be more open to share their expert knowledge and experience. Or, even combined workshops together with some university or training institutions would be helpful to disseminate TA know-how.

ELINOR: to be more open . . . online for instance?

TOMAS: Well, digital transformation and the pandemic challenged TA's model in the sense that it needs to be adapted to this new context. A global network is a must to speed up this adaptation process towards a more digitally inclusive TA model for the next generation of entrepreneurs.

ROBERTA: Absolutely online!!! Kindergartens, high schools, teacher training programmes. I just finished my PhD and my final proposition was a whole higher education teacher training programme based on human development using the TA approach.

BERRBIZNE: yes, and not only in formal education settings but business and other social settings as well.

NATALIA: I believe TA should explore its essence even deeper and find ways to apply it as a tool for the new "Gig-Economy", where self-employed people will certainly need a Team within which they can learn.

BETH: That is right Natalia. In an ideal there would be a next step after the degree programme that doesn't take form in an academic scenario; perhaps a space where alumni can come together to work, share, and learn. A space, where resources and mentorship is made available but as a business and personal service. This space could perhaps incorporate professional and personal developmental, accredited courses as well but above all it should encourage the continuation of teamwork, shared learning, and development.

DEO: in a sense everything can be *teamacademized*. All levels of education from Primary to Secondary to University can adopt this learning approach and all University programmes, including business and non-business programmes can adopt this. The work life in established organizations can adopt this approach as well by becoming learning organizations as well. Now with COVID, TA practitioners should take advantage of the availability of digital communications and open more collaboration opportunities around the Globe.

AINHOA: yes! A more digital, multilocal and present model than ever. Acknowledging diversity and fostering inclusivity. Making sure that the collective good and human growth is at the centre of the model allowing transformation from a people centred perspective. The Team Academy model values both team and individual perspectives as well as the community as the space for collective growth, the next step is to make sure that the team companies and projects spinning off the community remain responsible and aligned with a triple impact formula. It also needs to make sure that the teampreneurs remain not only active and participatory but challenge themselves to become leaders in their project and in their communities influencing the positive transformation of the global ecosystem.

BERRBIZNE: more open, people-focused, not only in academic settings, digital, multilocal, looking at diversity, inclusivity and community transformation and impact, but always keeping its values and principles at the centre. Thanks everyone for your contributions. It has been a pleasure to talk to you.

As is quite often the case, at the end of our discussions in this book, the last one of the series, we were left with more questions to consider about the future of TA and the contexts and settings in which we will see *teamacademians* operating next. Rather than being the end of the story, this is very much part of the journey. Book 1: *Team Academy in Entrepreneurship Education* in this series explores the underpinning philosophy of TA, where it began and how it relates to the broader team coaching and entrepreneurial learning work taking place. In book 2: *Team Academy in Practice* we move into what TA is in practice, exploring research and narratives from those in the field who are working with and developing academic TA-based programmes of study. Book 3: *Team Academy: Leadership and Teams* considers how leadership and the concept of teams emerge and are defined in the TA model. And in this final book, Book 4: *Team Academy in Diverse Settings*, we have explored TA as it appears outside of traditional TA-based settings, considering how TA might work in industry, schools, communities of practice, and beyond, and the legacy that it has left in learners and practitioners. There are many more stories to be told, and certainly more research to be done into this emergent model. Join us to further the conversation!

Index

Note: Page numbers in italics indicate a figure and page numbers in bold indicate a table on the corresponding page.

Printed in the United States
by Baker & Taylor Publisher Services